TCP/IP Over ATM

A No-Nonsense
Internetworking Guide

ISBN 0-13-768599-8

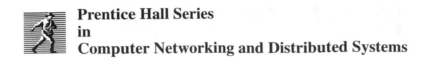

**Prentice Hall Series
in
Computer Networking and Distributed Systems**

Radia Perlman, Series Editor

TCP/IP OVER ATM

A No-Nonsense
Internetworking Guide

Berry Kercheval

To join a Prentice Hall PTR Internet
mailing list, point to:

http://www.prenhall.com/mail_lists/

Prentice Hall PTR
Upper Saddle River, NJ 07458

Library of Congress Cataloging-in-Publication Data

Kercheval, Berry.
     TCP/IP over ATM : a no-nonsense internetworking guide / Berry
Kercheval.
        p. cm.
     Includes bibliographical references and index.
     ISBN 0-13-768599-8
     1. TCP/IP (Computer network protocol)   2. Asynchronous transfer
mode.   3. Internetworking (Telecommunication) I. Title.
     TK5105.585.K47   1997
     004.6'6--dc21   97-42090
                                      CIP

Editorial/production supervision: *Dawn Speth White*
Cover design director: *Jerry Votta*
Cover designer: *Talar Agasyan*
Manufacturing manager: *Alexis R. Heydt*
Marketing manager: *Miles Williams*
Acquisitions editor: *Mary Franz*
Editorial assistant: *Noreen Regina*

 ©1998 by Prentice Hall PTR
Prentice-Hall, Inc.
A Simon & Schuster Company
Upper Saddle River, NJ 07458

Prentice Hall books are widely used by corporations and government agencies
for training, marketing, and resale.

The publisher offers discounts on this book when ordered in bulk quantities.
For more information, contact: Corporate Sales Department, Phone: 800-382-3419;
Fax: 201-236-7141; E-mail: corpsales@prenhall.com; or write: Prentice Hall PTR,
Corp. Sales Dept., One Lake Street, Upper Saddle River, NJ 07458.

AOL and America Online are service marks of America Online, Inc. AT&T is a trademark of AT&T. Adobe and
Adobe Type Manager are trademarks of Adobe Systems Incorporated. Cisco and Cisco Systems are registered
trademarks of Cisco Systems, Inc. DEC, Digital, Digital Equipment Corporation, AltaVista, and Vax are trade-
marks of Digital Equipment Corporation. Encyclopaedia Britannica is a trademark of Encyclopaedia Britannica,
Inc. ForeRunner and Fore Systems are registered trademarks of FORE Systems, Inc. Hewlett-Packard and
Afterburner are trademarks of Hewlett-Packard Company. Pacific Bell is a trademark of the Pacific Telesis
Group. Prodigy is a trademark of Prodigy Services Corporation. SPARC is a registered trademark of SPARC
International, Inc. Products using the SPARC trademarks are based on an architecture developed by Sun Micro-
systems, Inc. Sprint is a trademark of Sprint Communications Company, L.P. Sun and Solaris are trademarks of
Sun Microsystems, Inc. UNIX and X Window System are registered trademarks of The Open Group. USPS and
United States Postal Service are trademarks of the United States Postal Service. Xerox is a registered trademark
of Xerox Corporation. All other brand or product-specific names are trademarks of their respective owners.

Printed in the United States of America
10 9 8 7 6 5 4 3 2 1

ISBN 0-13-768599-8

Prentice-Hall International (UK) Limited, *London*
Prentice-Hall of Australia Pty. Limited, *Sydney*
Prentice-Hall Canada Inc., *Toronto*
Prentice-Hall Hispanoamericana, S.A., *Mexico*
Prentice-Hall of India Private Limited, *New Delhi*
Prentice-Hall of Japan, Inc., *Tokyo*
Simon & Schuster Asia Pte. Ltd., *Singapore*
Editora Prentice-Hall do Brasil, Ltda., *Rio de Janeiro*

*I never understood why so many writers
dedicate books to their spouses
until I wrote a book myself.*

Now I get it.

This book is dedicated to my wife, Alene.

Contents

Preface

A lot of literature about ATM seems to focus on the wonderful things that will happen when the whole world uses it, but few talk much about how to run today's networks over it. Since the recent explosive growth of the collection of IP networks that we call the Internet has made it pretty clear that TCP/IP is here to stay, I thought it would be a good idea for a book: to discuss ATM in the context of IP.

One problem in writing a book is deciding what to put in and what to leave out. There's so much data on ATM lying around that if I put it all in, this book's size would rival that of the *Encyclopædia Britannica*. That would make my publisher unhappy.

On the other hand, I could just say "ATM is a networking technology that hooks computers together. It's cool" and be done, but then you'd just read the whole book in the store and not buy it. That would make my publisher unhappy too.

So somewhere in between is a happy median. The problem is, that for every person out there, that happy median is in a different place. You probably want more nitty-gritty technical information than your boss does and less than the people who report to you do.

So here's what I've tried to do: I'm trying to aim this book at people who are familiar with networking in general, but who don't know much about ATM. You want to know how things work in some detail, but not so much detail that "bits" get in the way of concepts.

That's what I've tried to do. If you need to build a LAN Emulation server, or put UNI signaling into a router, you won't get *all* of the information to do it here. What you *will* get is a pretty good idea of how LAN Emulation or UNI signaling works and where to go to learn more.

I've tried to keep the tone of the book informal, yet accurate, since *I* like to read that kind of book. On the other hand, I feel a need to apologize for the unavoidable ragout of acronyms. Any field has its jargon, and networking has many special terms and acronyms. One of the hardest initial barriers to learning about ATM for me was the *new* set of acronyms I had to learn; since ATM's standards for the most part come out of the telecommunications industry and not from the more familiar data networking community, they tend to use a different set of names for everything. I've put everything I can think of into the glossary. Put a bookmark there as you read the book; it will help.

There's a fair amount of detail on protocols, packet formats and the like, which helps to illustrate how devices get information back and forth, and which can help you if you have to dig out a network sniffer and decode the raw cells to find out why the net is down—something I've done more than once!

I should point out that since the Internet and ATM is evolving in, well, Internet time,[1] some of the information in this book may be out-of-date by the time you read it. I hope the basics of how things work will remain stable, whatever happens to the fine details. I've tried to be clear about what versions of standards I'm referencing, as well as to provide pointers for what may be more up-to-date on-line information. On-line data changes rapidly, though, and World Wide Web URLs are not guaranteed to be accurate indefinitely.

In particular, I've avoided putting in much information about specific equipment and manufacturers. I don't want to make recommendations of what to buy since the market *will* have changed by the time you read this; but the *way* ATM works will stay the same.

A word about timeliness: This is a field that is rapidly changing. Some of the information in this book takes the form of World Wide Web URLs, the "Uniform Resource Locators" that allow access to web pages. Whether they are still valid when you go to type them into your browser is something I cannot control. If you have trouble accessing any of them, try using one of the many search engines to look for the topic; you may find that the keepers of the data just rearranged their files and gave what you're looking for a new name. On the other

---

[1] Internet time is like dog years—an Internet year seems to go by a lot faster than a "real" year.

hand, some of these URLs will just be bogus after awhile; I'm sorry about that, but I feel it's better to give a lot of pointers, some of which will be useful, than give none at all.

I would like to acknowledge the invaluable assistance of Steve Walters, Radia Perlman, John S. Swenson and J. Bryan Lyles, without whom this book would have been a lot less accurate and interesting.

And, of course, nothing in this book should be regarded as the official position of Xerox Corporation, my current employer. In particular, any mention of specific products is made only to illustrate a point or to provide examples and should in no way be construed as an endorsement (or otherwise) of any product by Xerox. They may or may not wish to endorse products, but I am not their spokesperson!

Here's a sketch of what the rest of the book is up to:

Chapter 1: Introduction, including a discussion of standards organizations relevant to ATM and TCP/IP.

Chapter 2: TCP/IP. A brief introduction to the TCP/IP protocol suite for those that are not familiar with it.

Chapter 3: SONET and other physical media. How bits get carried at high speed over various links.

Chapter 4: ATM. How ATM itself works. Cells, switches, virtual circuits, signaling, and so on.

Chapter 5: Management. SNMP, ILMI, and ATM routing.

Chapter 6: Classical IP over ATM. The IETF's way.

Chapter 7: LAN Emulation. The ATM Forum's way.

Chapter 8: Multicast, or how can you send packets to more than one place at a time?

Chapter 9: Traffic Management. ABR, UBR, QoS, RSVP flow control.

Chapter 10: How to make it fast. Just plugging in an ATM card isn't enough; you've got to tune everything up.

Chapter 11: Research Topics. A sampling of what is under active development. The chapter most likely to be out of date when this book is published, let alone five years from now.

I'll close with a bibliography, glossary, index, and pointers to more information on—where else?—the Internet.

Introduction

ATM is a buzzword that's being heard a lot these days, and it doesn't seem to mean "Automatic Teller Machine," "Adobe Type Manager," or even "Amateur Telescope Maker." In the context of computer networking it means "Asynchronous Transfer Mode" and is a new, emerging, and powerful technology.

ATM does not use a shared medium like Ethernet or FDDI. A connection through an ATM network between two hosts sending 155 Mbit to each other does not mean that no one else can send; two other hosts could easily send the same amount of data back and forth. This can be a great advantage in modern multimedia-capable networks that transport multiple streams of megabyte video.

ATM was chosen by CCITT (the international standards body, see Section 1.4.1) as the basis for the Broadband Integrated Services Digital Network (B-ISDN). This is a broadband version of the perhaps more familiar ISDN. An *Integrated Services* network means that the same network is used to carry all types of traffic: voice, data, video, whatever. All the types of data streams are *integrated* into one network. B-ISDN is a *broadband* version of this kind of network. In this context, broadband means high-speed; it comes from the terms in cable television: a video signal carried as a single signal in a cable is called baseband since the band of frequencies used can come from the base of the spectrum, but if multiple signals are modulated and fed together into a cable it is called broadband, since it uses a broad band of frequencies for all of the channels.

ATM uses the high-speed optical-fiber networking technology called
SONET. One of the nice features of using a high-speed WAN technology in a local
setting is that when local ATM nets are interconnected with public ATM nets, no
degradation of service is seen. This is good news for new bandwidth-hungry
applications like digital audio/video, virtual reality, and medical imaging.

ATM is particularly exciting for multimedia applications since it offers so
much bandwidth. Video in particular is a massive consumer of bandwidth. Consider an stream of ordinary NTSC video. (NTSC is the video standard used in the
United States, similar [but different] to PAL and SECAM in other countries.)

NTSC specifies 30 frames per second (glossing over fields and interlacing)
of about 640×480 pixels (which makes very nice looking video indeed!). If we use
one byte per pixel, we get

$$640 \times 480 \times 30 \times 8 \; = \; 73{,}728{,}000$$

or nearly 74 Mbit/sec! Compression techniques such as MPEG can reduce this
quite a bit, of course, but even so, consider High-Definition TV (HDTV). The new
digital system will just have even larger frames, exacerbating the video bandwidth problem despite compression.

ATM is built with the idea of *bandwidth reservations*, so that when an
application needs, say, a 12 Mbit/sec connection for a stream of MPEG video, it
can ask for it and rely on it being available once granted. Parameters for quality
of service (QoS) can be specified, so that data streams with hard limits on delay
can specify that their packets need to get there soon or they're worthless (how
useful is frame 123 of a movie when you've already shown frame 329?), while simple bulk data transfers can say, "Don't mind me, I can wait, as long as I get there."

1.1 The OSI Reference Model

I have to say a few words about the OSI reference model shown in Figure 1-1.

The model was developed as a way to apportion the work on the OSI protocols into different committees. This is not a diagram of how code must be written.
Not all of the layers have to exist in any given implementation; it's not even
really necessary to be able to identify the layers in the code. In some cases,
implementing a strict layered interface can actually slow the implementation
down substantially. If a coder realizes that in this implementation, layer N
doesn't actually do anything, why, its *OK* to leave it out! Really!

Sometimes, of course, the layers are good. If you're putting several protocols
on top of a single data link, such as XNS and TCP/IP, then it makes good sense to
have a defined interface to the datalink layer *in that system design*. Another system might be better off tightly coupling the layers.

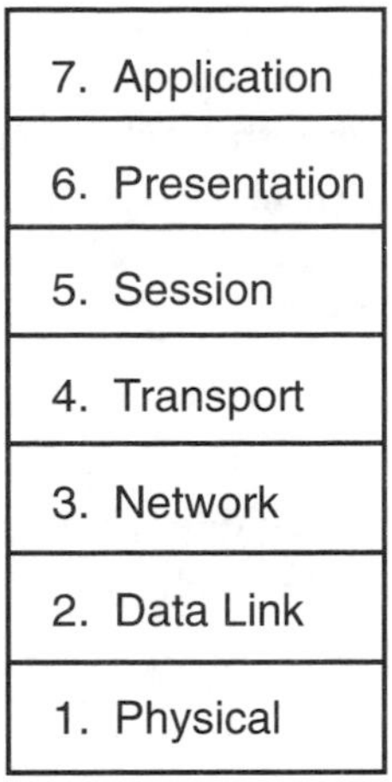

```
+------------------+
| 7. Application   |
+------------------+
| 6. Presentation  |
+------------------+
| 5. Session       |
+------------------+
| 4. Transport     |
+------------------+
| 3. Network       |
+------------------+
| 2. Data Link     |
+------------------+
| 1. Physical      |
+------------------+
```

Figure 1-1. Obligatory OSI reference model.

So the model can be used as a useful tool for thinking about the architecture of a system, but it should not be used as a Procrustean bed that designs have to be forced to fit. It's an abstraction, not a straightjacket.

For all that, use of the terms "layer two" and "layer three" are widespread in the networking community. Layer two is named the *data link* layer. It takes packets from layer three and arranges for their bits to be fed into the physical network in the appropriate way. In an Ethernet, it would build Ethernet frames and transmit them onto the cable, using the appropriate timing and collision detection. In an ATM network it would chop the packet into ATM cells and send them out on the correct virtual circuit.

Layer three is called the *network layer*; it is responsible for getting packets to their destination. Routing takes place at this level—choosing a path through the network so the packet will make it all of the way.

The next layer up, the *transport layer*, is where the actual protocols live. This is the realm of TCP, for instance. (Most people don't think that TCP/IP fits the OSI model very well; this bothers people of the OSI religion, but TCP/IP disciples say "It works, so sue us.")

1.2 What's a Public Network?

A "public network," as compared to a privately operated one, is operated for the benefit of the general public. Public networks must typically accept any paying customer that desires the services offered. The telephone network is an example of this. Telephone companies are regulated by the government and must provide service to anyone able to pay the monthly service charge.

ATM, or B-ISDN, is supposed to bring a public data network to the customers.

Anyone who wishes computer network services would be able to connect their machine—much like plugging in a telephone—and be able to communicate with others. Standardization of interfaces and protocols would ensure that any computer could talk to any other, just as today any telephone can call any other telephone, anywhere in the world.

To ensure that the benefits of this scenario are achievable, some things are necessary. One is that what constitutes "good behavior" must be specified, measured, and ensured. It should impossible for a few "bandwidth hogs" to monopolize the network. ATM's QoS features help provide this.

Also, the resources should be allocated "fairly." What "fair" means is a matter of some controversy, but one proposal is that customers should pay for what they get and get what they pay for; in other words, a usage-sensitive pricing scheme: The more resources you use the more you pay. For example, a user needing assured bandwidth with bounded delay for a video conference might be willing to pay more than someone doing an overnight bulk data transfer with no hard requirements other than "it should be done by morning." ATM's ability to specify different classes of network traffic make such pricing feasible.

Some people object to any kind of usage-sensitive pricing, arguing that "unlimited" free bandwidth is what made the Internet great, but the Internet was never "free"; the charges were often hidden from the users, and typically not usage-sensitive, but they were there. Further, usage-sensitive pricing helps avoid the "tragedy of the commons" discussed in Chapter 9.

1.3 Networking Basics

Here is a brief introduction to net basics to make sure we're speaking the same language.

When a computer on the Internet needs to send data to another computer, it bundles up the data it needs to send into one or more *packets*. It labels the packet with the *addresses* of itself and the destination computer and then sends it out on its local network.

Then, a specialized computer called a *router* receives the packets, examines the destination address in each one, and decides which of its *links* the packet should be sent down.

Eventually the packets arrive on the destination network and are received by the destination computer, which feeds them into its *protocol stack* for processing and eventual delivery to the application expecting the data.

1.4 Standards Bodies

Standards are the grease in the wheels of technology. They insure that when you buy a toaster and take it home, the plug on the end will fit into the power sockets in your kitchen, that when you rent a movie, your VCR can play it, and when you plug a computer into a network, it will be able to communicate with other computers.

There are many standards relevant to TCP/IP and ATM. In this section we will take a look at some of the organizations that produce the standards and how they are created.

If you really want to know what the standard says there is no substitute for reading the standard itself instead of a summary. Many times the summary is perfectly adequate, but for picky little implementation details, the standard itself has the final say. Unfortunately, many standards documents tend to be rife with acronyms and specialized terms. It takes a bit of practice to get the hang of it.

1.4.1 The International Telecommunications Union

The International Telecommunication Union (ITU) is a specialized agency of the United Nations that serves to standardize and regulate all aspects of global telecommunications. You have the ITU to thank (at least in part) for the fact that you can dial up a fax machine on the other side of the world and expect not only that the phone call will go through, but that the fax machines will be able exchange data in a useful way.

The ITU sees its mission as having three broad aspects. First, they promote the development of telecommunications. Second, they offer technical assistance to developing countries so as to extend telecommunications technologies worldwide. Finally, they encourage a broad approach to telecommunications in the global economy.

At last count (February 1997) there were 187 member states and 406 other members (companies, network operators, broadcasters, and regional and international organizations).

There are several sectors of activity. One is the *Radiocommunications Sector*, which regulates international use of radio frequencies.

Another is the *Telecommunication Development Sector*, which promotes the use of modern telecommunications networks in developing countries.

The sector of most interest for us is the *Telecommunication Standardization Sector*, also called ITU-T.

The work of the ITU-T is broken up into *study groups*, each of which is assigned a number. The current list of study groups is shown in Table 1-1.

(The sharp-eyed reader will notice that Study Groups 1 and 14 are absent. This is the list supplied by the ITU, and presumably the groups either never were created or have been disbanded for some reason.)

Table 1-1. ITU Study Groups.

Number	Study Group Name
2	Network and service operation
3	Tariff and accounting principles
4	TMN and network maintenance
5	Protection against electromagnetic environment effects
6	Outside plant
7	Data networks and open system communications
8	Characteristics of telematic systems
9	Television and sound transmission
10	Languages and general software aspects for telecommunication systems
11	Signaling requirements and protocols
12	End-to-end transmission performance of networks and terminals
13	General network aspects
15	Transport networks, systems, and equipment
16	Multimedia services and systems

We're most interested in the work of Study Group 13. This is the group that studies general network issues.

The final "output" of the study groups is a series of Recommendations. These are the actual standards documents. They too are divided into Series, each of which has a letter. The current series are shown in Table 1-2.

Here we see where various recommendations fit. The ATM address standard is E.164, which fits into series E, "Overall network operation." SONET (or SDH) is discussed in Series G, and the "V.34" modem you may use must follow the recommendations in, yes, V.34 from series V "Data communication over the telephone network."

ITU Documents can be found on-line in various places, as described in Appendix A. Some are free (meeting schedules, lists of documents, etc.) but most cost money (a major source of revenue for the organization). A CD-ROM of all ITU-T recommendations is available either as a one-time purchase or on a subscription basis. It is pricey but indispensable for serious telecommunications researchers and implementors.

Alternatively, the ITU has an on-line subscription service that you can sign up for; new recommendations will be sent automatically.

Table 1-2. ITU Recommendation Series.

Series	Name
A	Organization of the work of the ITU-T
B	Means of expression (definitions, symbols, classification)
C	General telecommunication statistics
D	General tariff principles
E	Overall network operation, telephone service, service operation, and human factors
F	Telecommunication services other than telephone
G	Transmission systems and media, digital systems, and networks
H	Line transmission of nontelephone signals
I	Integrated Services Digital Networks (ISDN)
J	Transmission of sound programme and television signals
K	Protection against interference
L	Construction, installation, and protection of cable and other elements of outside plant
M	Maintenance: transmission systems, telephone circuits, telegraphy, facsimile, ...
N	Maintenance: international sound programme and television transmission circuits
O	Specifications of measuring equipment
P	Telephone transmission quality, telephone installations, local line networks
Q	Switching and signaling
R	Telegraph transmission
S	Telegraph services terminal equipment
T	Terminal characteristics and higher layer protocols for telematics
U	Telegraph switching
V	Data communication over the telephone network
X	Data networks and open system communication
Z	Programming languages

1.4.2 ATM Forum

The ATM Forum was formed in 1991 by a group of manufacturers of ATM equipment who, not unreasonably, wanted to foster the adoption of ATM. The plan was to provide a "forum" for discussion and agreement on specifications for ATM. The ATM Forum is divided into a Technical Committee, and three Market Awareness Committees for North America, Europe, and Asia and the Pacific. There is also an Enterprise Network Roundtable.

The Market Awareness Committees encourage education about ATM. The Enterprise Network Roundtable is formed of end-users of ATM equipment and provides a way for them to have input into the processes, so that ATM doesn't become another committee-designed standard that everyone agrees is pretty but no-one wants to use.

The Technical Committee is the one we are most interested in, though, because it is here that the standards are built. The committee's work includes selecting existing standards, resolving differences when there are conflicts, and recommending new standards when there is a need.

Major works by the Technical Committee include the specifications for LAN Emulation (see Chapter 7) and the User-Network Interface (UNI).

The "Anchorage Accord," named for the location of the meeting where it was ratified, outlines 60 standards that make up what is needed to build a complete ATM network. It also lays out how interoperability will be ensured so that network builders can purchase and install the best gear they can find, confident that it will all work together.

Currently[1] there are 215 principal members, including nearly all of the major telecommunications and computer manufacturers.

1.4.3 Internet Engineering Task Force

The group that works on standards for the Internet is the Internet Engineering Task Force (IETF). The IETF is chartered by the Internet Society to be an open forum for anyone interested in participating in the development of the Internet architecture.

In distinct contrast to the ITU and ATM Forum, IETF meetings are completely open. Any interested person can pay the nominal registration fee and attend meetings. All persons attending a meeting speak as individuals, not as representatives of a country or company. No voting per se takes place; as Dave Clark has said, "We reject kings, presidents, and voting. We believe in rough consensus and running code" [Borsook 95]. In other words, if you want to propose a standard for adoption by the IETF, bringing a working example, instead of a paper description, counts for a lot. In IETF meetings, it is common to hear the

---

[1] From the ATM Forum WWW page (http://www.atmforum.com) as of 17 May 1997.

chairperson ask "Do we have rough consensus that...?" If nobody screams "NO!", then it "passes."

At first, sounds like a terrible way to run things, but in practice it works quite well, much to the dismay of folks associated with more formal standards bodies. A detailed presentation of how it works can be found in [Ramsøy 1995].

The group has grown a lot since the first meeting in January 1986 at Linkabit in San Diego with 15 attendees. The 38th meeting was held in Memphis Tennessee in April 1997; 1321 people registered for it. (The 37th meeting in December 1996 in San Jose, CA, was even better attended: 1993 attendees. Being held in Silicon Valley had something to do with it.)

Structure of the IETF

The IETF is divided into *areas*, each of which has several *working groups*. Each area has an Area Director who is a member of the Internet Engineering Steering Group or IESG. A list of the areas of the IETF is shown in Table 1-3.

The Internet Architecture Board (IAB) provides general guidance on the architecture of the Internet and provides a recourse for folks unhappy about the actions of the IETF. The Internet Assigned Numbers Authority or IANA is responsible for assigning numbers—for instance, when a new service needs a code to identify it, IANA decides what it should be.

All of these groups are chartered by the Internet Society.

The documents produced by the IETF are called Requests for Comments (RFCs). The name stems from the early days of the Internet, when no one really knew what they were doing. It became common practice to write up a proposal and put it out for comments; eventually the name "Request for Comments" stuck and they began to be organized and archived.

The general procedure for creating one is as follows.[2] Members of a working group decide that a document is needed for a certain purpose, and they write one. This is submitted to the IETF as an Internet Draft (ID). IDs expire after six months and are not archived. Not only that, but it is strictly forbidden for anyone to reference an Internet Draft in a paper (without "work in progress" disclaimers) or for a vendor to claim compliance with one. (Obviously folks working on early implementations can *assert* compliance, but these "bleeding edge" developers know and accept the risk that the "standard-to-be" may change out from under them.)

The working group, which consists of everyone on the planet who cares enough to subscribe to the working group's electronic mailing list, discuss and perhaps revise the draft. If it is considered good, the working-group chair asks the RFC Editor to issue it as an RFC.

---

[2] For some reason I feel like I'm writing the Internet version of the section in all U.S. civics textbooks called, "How a Bill Becomes Law." No Gates jokes, please.

Some, but not all, RFCs are standards; documents that are intended to become standards are termed "standards track." The RFC moves through stages of Proposed Standard, Draft Standard, and the final stage, Internet Standard. No, I tell a lie, the *real* final stage is "obsoleted by..." a newer Internet Standard. Obsolete RFCs are kept around for historical interest, but are marked as obsolete.

There is a tradition that a humorous RFC is published every All Fools Day—April First. Classic examples are RFC 1149, *Standard for the transmission of IP datagrams on avian carriers* (i.e., carrier pigeons) and RFC 1605, *SONET to Sonnet Translation* (which treats the compressing of SONET frames into English sonnets of 14 lines of iambic pentameter).

1.4.4 Mini-Glossary

Here is a short glossary of terms used in this book. There is much more in the glossary at the back of this book or in [Malkin 1993], but these terms are important, used much in this book and sometimes confused with each other. I'm sorry about the alphabet soup in the book; I've tried to hold it down but eliminating it altogether would be difficult, and actually unfair. Most of the documents on ATM are just as bad, if not worse. I hope you'll be prepared in some degree to do battle with the standards on your own after reading this book, so you need to get used to the jargon a bit; I'll be gentle.

A *bit* is a unit of data, either a 0 or 1. A *byte* is usually 8 bits. An *octet* is *always* 8 bits. The term octet came into use in the early days of the Internet because some machines such as PDP-10s and Honeywells didn't have 8-bit bytes (or bytes at all in some cases; in some cases the minimum addressable unit of memory was the 36-bit word). This may seem strange in today's almost universal usage of 8-bit bytes, but for the most part, network engineers try to avoid making assumptions about the computers hooked to the net. I will use the terms byte and octet interchangeably in this book, but if you dive into the RFCs and other standards you will see the term *octet* used a lot.

A *packet* is any unit of data sent across some kind of network. It is usually used to refer to data at the application level (TCP packets, IP packets, etc.).

A *PDU* or "*Protocol Data Unit*" is a packet, but in what Malkin and Parker call "internationalstandardscommitteespeak."

A *frame* is packet from the network layer encapsulated with required headers and trailers for the physical medium. An IP packet with an Ethernet header attached becomes an Ethernet frame.

A *cell* is the 53-byte fixed-size packet used by ATM.

A *datagram* is a self-contained unit of data that includes enough information to be routed from its source to its destination. A cell is not a datagram, because it relies on the routing setup in the switching network for its routing; the cell itself contains only the identifier of the virtual circuit to the next switch.

IP packets are datagrams because they include source and destination addresses that are sufficient for any intermediate router to speed the packet on its way.

Two terms that are important to get straight are *bridge* and *router*. Both forward data between networks, but using different techniques.

A *bridge* uses information from the datalink layer such as Ethernet. It joins two or more physical segments of network into a single logical network as viewed from the network layer. For example, my ISDN bridge connects the Ethernet segment at my home to an Ethernet segment at the Palo Alto Research Center (PARC) called "HomeNet." None of the applications I run can tell the difference between being at PARC or at home (aside from ISDN being slower than Ethernet, of course).

A *router*, on the other hand, uses network layer information to do its forwarding. Routers must look at network layer packets, like IP, and decide how to forward them by consulting their routing tables.

On the third hand, a *switch* is neither a bridge or a router. It accepts packets and distributes them to destinations according to fixed rules, usually in hardware. ATM networks are built using "ATM switches." If it helps to think of them as very specialized datalink layer routers, well, that's close enough to correct for our purposes.

Different standard bodies use different words for "computer." Host, node, end station, end-system, workstation machine and so on are pretty much equivalent. End-station is favored by the ITU, for instance, because it doesn't have any connotations that imply a general-purpose computer. An ATM end-station could be such a computer, but it could just as well be a digital camera, an X-Ray machine in a hospital or the X-Ray viewer in a doctor's office, or even an automated teller machine in a bank (imagine, an ATM ATM!).

Then there's "entity," which can refer to a computer, a module in a computer, a process, or a program.

I'll tend to use "host" or "computer" in discussions. Some of the symbols that will appear in diagrams throughout the book are shown in Figure 1-2.

 ATM Switch

 End Station

 Server

Figure 1-2. Symbols used in figures.

Sometimes a packet must have additional information sent with it to allow it to be properly handled by the network. The technique of "wrapping" a packet in such additional data is called *encapsulation*.

Next, after a tour of TCP/IP we can dive into the world of ATM. Don't forget to check the glossary frequently!

CHAPTER 2

IP, the Internet Protocol, and Its Friends and Relations

A *whirlwind tour of IP and related protocols*

$\mathbf{T}$he heart of today's Internet is IP, the Internet Protocol. This is the foundation protocol for data transmission on the Internet. In this chapter we take a look at the history and workings of this protocol family and some of the services that it provides.

2.1 What *Is* the Internet, Anyway? And How Big Is It?

The global collection of interconnected networks using the TCP/IP protocol family is called the Internet. What exactly "network" means in this context is often unclear. If you have a little Ethernet in your office with a few machines on it, that's a "network" or more precisely, a LAN segment. If you hook it to another Ethernet in the next office with a router, you have...a bigger network. You[1] have just constructed an "internet," with a small "i". Eventually, the network in your building may connect to an Internet Service Provider and suddenly you are on the Internet with a big "I."

---

[1] or your hardworking system administrator.

What this means is that if you are "on the Internet," everywhere that you can get to with, say, Telnet, the World Wide Web (WWW), Gopher, or File Transfer Protocol (FTP) is the Internet.

Now, this is actually a fuzzy definition. Pinning it down is surprisingly hard. Consider:

- Are PCs connected to online services like AOL or Prodigy on the Internet? Well, they can use the WWW, fetch files, and so on, so some folks would say yes. But you cannot send IP packets to them—they use a proprietary protocol to relay these connections through the computers at AOL or Prodigy, so others can argue just as validly that they are not "on" the Internet at all.
- Are computers behind corporate firewalls on the Internet? Well, they can sometimes make connections outward, but no one can connect inward, so most people would say that they are *sort of* on the Internet.

These problems make an exact definition of the Internet so hard as to be nearly pointless, at least in part because no one will agree on the definitions.

This also makes it very hard to determine how "big" the Internet is. Do we count users? Hosts? Networks? Domains? Routes? Or something else?

Whatever definition may be used, no one denies that the Internet has grown. From the original four hosts in 1969 to today's millions, growth has been explosive. Mark Lottor and the Network Wizards[2] attempt to determine the size of the Internet by taking a sampling of host names from the nameservers and attempting to contact them using ping. The latest results from July 1997 show that there are *probably* at least 20 million hosts on the Internet (Figure 2-1).

So far, whatever definition is used, the historical data fit an exponential growth curve quite well.

2.2 History of the Internet

The roots of the Internet trace back to the 1960s when the U.S. Department of Defense decided to fund network development through the Advanced Research Projects Agency (ARPA). The consulting firm of Bolt, Beranek, and Newman (BBN) was chosen to implement the network, and in 1969 ARPANET went online with four sites at the University of California, Los Angeles (UCLA), University of California, Santa Barbara (UCSB), the Stanford Research Institute (SRI), Menlo Park, CA, and the University of Utah, Salt Lake City.

---

[2] The latest data can be found at http://www.nw.com/

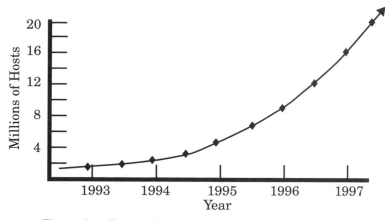

Figure 2-1. Recent Internet growth (per Network Wizards).

A design goal of ARPANET was robustness. Any given link or computer could quit operating, whether through nuclear attack or a backhoe cutting a trunk line, and the rest of the network should still operate.

In 1982, the Defense Communications Agency (DCA) and ARPA chose the Transmission Control Protocol (TCP) over IP to be the protocol used for ARPANET, and thus, for the Internet.

It was at about this time that "Internet" began to be used a term for an interconnected set of networks, specifically those using TCP/IP.

In 1983, the ARPA-funded Computer Systems Research Group at the University of California's Berkeley campus released 4.2BSD, a version of Unix for the Digital Equipment Corporation's VAX minicomputer. This was the first widely-available implementation of TCP/IP and has proven to be very influential; many of today's TCP/IP implementations can trace their code directly to Berkeley.

In 1984 it became clear that the old method of keeping track of the hosts on the net was soon going to become unworkable. After all, there were almost a thousand hosts on the ARPANET! Where previously a master list of hosts periodically had to be fetched, a dynamically updated hierarchical service for mapping hostnames to addresses called the Domain Name System (DNS) was introduced. At this point, it began to be clear that soon it would be impossible to measure the size of the Internet, since the necessary information was now distributed worldwide, and if the growth continued, it would soon be updated faster than it could be queried.

The DNS system is organized, like so much in the computer world, hierarchically. At the top are the seven main *domains* administered by the Internet Network Information Center (InterNIC), which is a nonprofit organization funded by AT&T, the National Science Foundation (NSF), and Network Solutions, Inc. The original seven top-level domains are shown in Table 2-1. An orga-

Table 2-1. Top-level domains.

Domain	Purpose
.com	Commercial organizations
.edu	Educational organizations: colleges, universities and other schools
.gov	U.S. Government and government agencies
.net	Computers of network providers (the NIC, ISPs, etc.)
.org	Miscellaneous organizations
.mil	U.S. military organizations
.int	Intended for international organizations formed by treaties, such as the United Nations or NATO

nization can request a domain name to be assigned in one of these top-level domains; for example, Xerox Corporation has been assigned "xerox.com." The organization can then assign names within this domain as it wishes. Xerox, for instance assigns the domain "parc.xerox.com" to the Palo Alto Research Center, and their administrators can assign as many names within that domain as they wish (or that researchers need).

Other countries are assigned domains that start with their ISO country code. The United Kingdom of Great Britain and Northern Ireland uses ".uk", and La République Française uses ".fr". A national organization in each country manages name assignment there. (But entities outside the United States can get ".com" addresses, so don't assume ".com" means the U.S., though there is a ".us" domain.)

Because of name collisions in some domains, especially ".com", there is a great deal of controversy over the administration of these names, with calls for new top-level domains, auditing of the InterNIC, lawsuits flying hither and yon, and all kinds of mean and nasty stuff. It's interesting that what one might think is a purely technical problem of managing hostnames in a hierarchical manner turns into such a political morass.

A series of computers known as *nameservers* has been established that parallels the domain structure.[3] To figure out or *resolve* the IP address of a given host, one sends a request containing the name to one's local nameserver (assigned by the network administrator). It's much like calling Directory Assistance to obtain a phone number for a person you want to call, with the added benefit that instead of telling you that to look up Fred in Chicago you have to call

---

[3] It is a requirement that every domain have a designated nameserver. Some domains run their own, and some may choose to let their Internet Service Provider handle it.

Chicago Directory Assistance, DNS will call Chicago for you. Metaphorically speaking, that is.

   If the local nameserver doesn't know the address for the name asked about, the request is passed up to a higher server. So, for example, if I am working on dzur.parc.xerox.com and wish to resolve, say, ftp.x.org, my machine would ask the parc.xerox.com server (Figure 2-2). If it didn't know, it would ask the xerox.com server, and if that one didn't know either, it would ask a top-level .com server. The .com server might still not know the answer, but it *would* know the nameserver for .org, and would pass the request along to it. The .org server would then know x.org's server, since it knows the addresses of all of the .org servers, and eventually the answer would come back with the IP address of ftp.x.org, and I could get the latest cool X Window System games.

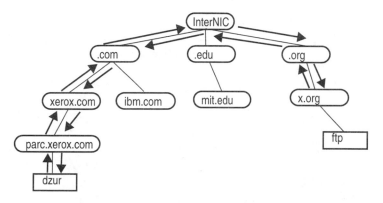

Figure 2-2. DNS tree structure and message flow.

   In 1987 the number of hosts passed ten thousand. The National Science Foundation (NSF) took over administration of the Internet, and in 1990, the ARPANET proper was dismantled, as it was no longer needed.

   Today there are more than 20 million hosts on the Internet; a number that is difficult to measure. The data in Figure 2-1 were obtained by querying a random sample of DNS servers and attempting to `ping` a random sample of the enumerated hosts. The figures are extrapolated from the results and have an unknown margin of error. This error tells us that the absolute values of the numbers are probably wrong, but since they use the same technique each time, the *trend* in the data is fairly accurate.

   But whatever the error, it's clear that the Internet is growing exponentially and has shown no sign of slowing down.

2.3 Overview of the Internet Protocols

Like any edifice, the foundation of the Internet protocol suite is the bottom layer, which sits on top of whatever transport being used, whether Ethernet, serial lines, FDDI, ATM, or carrier pigeons [RFC 1149]. This protocol provides transport of datagrams from one place to another, routing from network to network until it gets to its destination. It's called, appropriately enough, the Internet Protocol or IP (Figure 2-3).

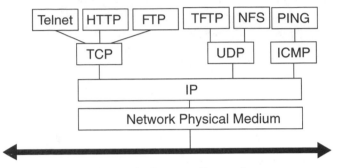

Figure 2-3. Internet Protocols.

IP provides no guarantee of delivery or ordering. That's left up to higher level protocols. The most popular one is the Transmission Control Protocol (TCP). TCP provides a reliable ordered byte-stream to applications. Services like Telnet, the WWW's HTTP, and electronic mail all use TCP.

Another higher level protocol is the User Datagram Protocol (UDP), which is a protocol for delivering datagrams to user processes. Examples of UDP "users" are the Trivial File Transfer Protocol (TFTP), often used by diskless machines to find their boot images, and the Network File System (NFS).

The Internet Control Message Protocol (ICMP) provides for various control and feedback mechanisms. Its most visible attributes are the Ping program and Traceroute. Ping sends "Echo Request" packets to hosts and expects to get back "Echo Reply." This is very useful for determining if a given machine is "up" or not.

If you send a message with a small "time to live," a router will send back a "Time Exceeded" error message. The traceroute program cleverly uses this to probe the route to a given destination, listing all the routers in the path and the round-trip time to get a packet there and back. This is extremely useful in diagnosing routing problems.

ICMP also provides feedback about the network. Messages such as "Host Unreachable" and the like allow a host to stop trying to send data to a place that's not going to get it.

2.4 Internet Addresses and Packet Formats

Every IP packet has a header at least 20 bytes long, containing two addresses, that of the source and that of the destination (Figure 2-4).

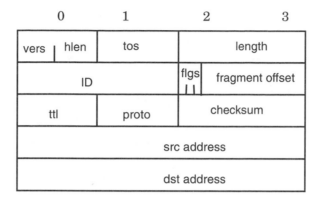

Figure 2-4. IP packet header.

IP addresses are 32 bits long, and are divided into two parts: the network number and the host number. Addresses are commonly written as four decimal numbers, one for each byte, separated by periods or dots. (Hence the term "dot-ted-decimal notation" seen in the RFCs.) Since 1 byte can hold numbers from 0 to 255, the addresses can range from 0.0.0.0 to 255.255.255.255.

The other fields in the header are:

- *vers*: the version of IP being used. Always 4 (unless the new IPv6 is being used; which is not yet widely deployed in the Internet).
- *hlen*: the length of this packet's header in 32-bit words. Usually 5, but IP packet headers can have optional parts that make it longer.
- *tos*: type of service. Specifies whether minimum delay, maximum throughput, maximum reliability, or minimize cost. As it turns out, this field is not much used and is usually set to zeros.
- *length*: the total length of the IP packet.
- *ID*: this field uniquely identifies the packet; used in fragmentation and reassembly.
- *flgs*: one bit is the "more fragments" flag, set in every fragment but the last.
- *Fragment Offset*: the offset of this packet's data in the original, unfragmented packet.
- *TTL*: time to live. This field is set by the sender and decremented each time the packet passes through a router. The packet is discarded when it reaches zero; this prevents packets caught in routing loops from being forwarded forever.

- *proto*: which upper layer protocol the data in this packet belongs to: TCP, UDP, ICMP, and so on.
- *checksum*: the complement of the 16-bit one's-complement sum of the headers. When a packet is received, the one's complement sum of the headers is calculated; this checksum is craftily designed to make a correctly received packet's header sum to all ones. Note that the data part of the packet is not checksummed at this layer.
- *addresses*: the IP addresses of the source and destination of this packet.

IP Addresses are divided into two parts, the network and host parts. Typically, a small network will be assigned a network part number, and the machines attached to it will be numbered from the range possible in the host part. If the host part is all ones, it's considered a local broadcast address and packets sent to that address should go to all hosts attached to the local network.

Addresses can be divided into classes according to how many bits of the 32 are allocated for the host part and for the network part (Figure 2-5).

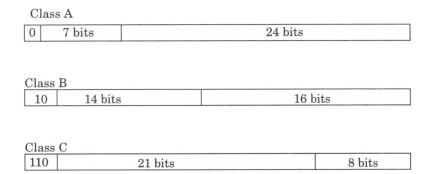

Figure 2-5. IP packet address formats.

If the network part is 8 bits, the network is called a "Class A Network." The original ARPANET was a class A network; all addresses looked like 10.x.y.z. Today, most class A networks belong to organizations that were early adopters of Internet technology, such as MIT (Net 18), Hewlett-Packard (Net 15) or Xerox (Net 13). Network 10 is now no longer in use and is one of the networks reserved for local use, disconnected from the Internet. Class A network parts can range from 1 to 127; the most significant bit is always a 0.

The addressing scheme is arranged so that if the two high-order bits in the address are "10", it's a class B address, and if the three high-order bits are "110", it's a class C address. Remembering how binary math works, this means that the first byte of a class A address can be from 1 to 127, that of a class B from 128 to 191, and of a class C from 192 to 223. (After 223, with three high bits set, we get into class D addresses, which are used in IP multicast and will be discussed later in Chapter 8. Four high bits set indicate Class E addresses, which are "reserved for further study.")

It's easy to imagine that Class F would start with five high bits, but in fact, no such address family has been standardized. (RFC1375 proposed some new network classes called F through H, but was never adopted as a standard.)

The important thing to note here is that, while there can be 2^{24} (or about 16 million) addresses *in* a class A address, there are only 127 total class A networks. Similarly, though there can be 2^{21} Class C networks, there can only be 256 hosts in each. With the recent explosive growth in the Internet, there is an increasing squeeze on IP addresses, with exhaustion of the address space forecast anywhere from "any day now" to "a few years away," depending on how pessimistic one feels. The "Next Generation" IP protocol, IP Version 6, is intended to address this (and other) problems with larger addresses.

2.5 The IP Protocol

IP is a *datagram protocol,* which means that there is no connection involved in delivery of packets, and that the packet contains enough information within itself to be routed all the way to the destination. The sending host just dumps the packet into the network and "hopes" that it arrives at its destination. Most of the time, when things are working, it does, and this turns out to be enough of a foundation to build quite a number of sophisticated protocols.

2.5.1 Routers

If the source and destination hosts are on the same local network, then the packet just goes from one to the other. If they are on different networks, though, the packet has to be forwarded to the other network.

A datagram protocol is like the post office. Make up a datagram, or letter, drop it into the network, or mailbox, and it eventually shows up in your friend's mailbox. If it's a local letter, the letter carrier could just take it down the street and drop it in the destination mailbox. If it goes to another town, though, it's taken to the local post office, where it's sorted, and a batch of letters for another town is sent along.

The network equivalent of the post office that sorts the letters is a *router.* Routers receive datagrams, look at the destination address, consult a *routing table* to determine where the datagram should be sent, and send it along. Eventually it arrives at a router at the destination, which sends the packet to the final host.

Since the Internet is very large and growing all the time (users are being added at a growth rate of about 85 percent per year [Quarterman 1996]) the information about which hosts are connected by which routers, and indeed, which routers are connected to each other, is changing constantly. Routers exchange this information using routing protocols, to keep their internal tables accurate. Considering that 85 percent annual growth and an estimated size of 20 million implies that a new host is being connected to the Internet every 2 seconds or so will give you an idea of how fast things change.

A detailed discussion of router technology could take the rest of this book, but fortunately there's already an excellent one. I recommend that interested readers consult [Perlman 1992].

2.5.2 Maximum Transmission Unit

Routers connect to each other using many different link technologies, everything from a telephone line with a modem on each end to gigabit ATM links. Different links allow different size packets. The largest legal packet size on an Ethernet, for instance, is 1500 bytes, while an ATM link using AAL5 could use about 65,528. (2^{16}–8, see Section 4.7.4 for an explanation of this number.) The size of the largest legal IP packet that can be sent on a given link is called the maximum transmission unit (MTU).

2.5.3 Fragments

So what happens when an 8000-byte packet arrives at a router and has to be sent along a link that has an MTU of 1500? IP allows packets to be broken into fragments, each piece of the original packet being wrapped in another IP packet of "legal" size for the outgoing link. IP fragmentation uses the identification field in the IP header to identify which packet a fragment belongs to and the fragment offset field to identify where in the packet this fragment goes.

The receiving host must buffer the fragments and reassemble them when all of the pieces arrive. (Fragments are never reassembled except in the final destination host.)

If a fragment comes to a router with a link with an even smaller MTU, then the fragment must be fragmented. Since each fragment's IP packet header carries the length of the fragment and its offset in the entire packet, reassembly is straightforward though tedious.

In any case, fragmenting and reassembling packets consume quite a number of resources. The receiving host must not only allocate a buffer in which to reassemble the packet and keep it around until all the fragments arrive, it must also somehow keep track of *which* fragments have arrived and *when*, and which are still outstanding, and periodically check on partial packets to see if it should give up and throw them away.

It's better to just avoid fragmentation altogether by sending packets of a size that can make it through the network without being fragmented [Kent 1987]. In order to do this, some TCP/IP stacks support "Path MTU Discovery"

[Mogul 1990] whereby they send a large packet with the "Don't Fragment" bit set and get back ICMP error messages from intermediate routers that say "Fragmentation is needed but I can't do it" and include the MTU of the next-hop network—the one that couldn't take the packet.

By reducing the packet size and trying again, eventually the minimum MTU of the complete path can be determined, and if all packets sent are no larger than that, fragmentation can be avoided for that connection. [Kent 1987] shows that this will lead to a performance gain—or, at least, avoiding fragmentation will avoid a performance loss.

2.6 TCP

With IP, we have a way of delivering data from computer to computer across the Internet—maybe. IP itself makes absolutely no guarantee that the data will actually be delivered. The strongest "promise" made by the network to the application program is "I will try my best to deliver these data, but if I drop the packet on the floor at some point, well, too bad."

So it is up to a higher layer protocol to impose sequencing and reliability on the stream of IP packets.

The protocol used to deliver reliable streams of data to applications is called the Transmission Control Protocol (TCP).

I am only going to give a brief summary of the operation of TCP here, so that the discussions that follow will make sense. For a thorough discussion of the ins and outs of TCP, IP, and the other IP protocols, see [Stevens 1994].

TCP is a connection-oriented protocol that provides a reliable byte stream to the applications using it. There are no record boundaries in TCP streams, and even the packet boundaries cannot be reliably determined by an application.

When using TCP, an application that wishes to communicate with another must first establish a connection to the other application. Once the connection is made, either side can send data until one decides to close down the connection.

TCP packets are carried as the data inside IP packets (Figure 2-6). The networking jargon word used for this is *encapsulated*. Think of a TCP packet being wrapped up and sealed into an IP "time capsule" that will be opened by the destination computer. This metaphor turns out to be apt, since intermediate routers don't need to look at the TCP headers at all; the IP header provides enough information to get from here to there.

A TCP packet header is shown in Figure 2-7. Right now, look at the bits in the fourth 32-bit word of the TCP header. This word is divided into four parts:

1. a 4-bit header length that gives the length of this TCP header in bytes. This is usually 20, the length of the mandatory header, unless there are options;

IP Hdr
TCP Hdr
Data
TCP Packet
IP Packet

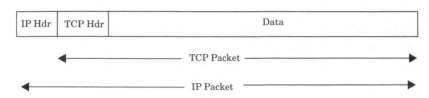

Figure 2-6. TCP packet encapsulated in an IP packet.

2. 6 bits that are not used;
3. 6 bits of flags: URG, ACK, PSH, RST, SYN, and FIN; and
4. a 16-bit window size.

A TCP packet with, say, the SYN flag bit set is said to be a *SYN packet*.

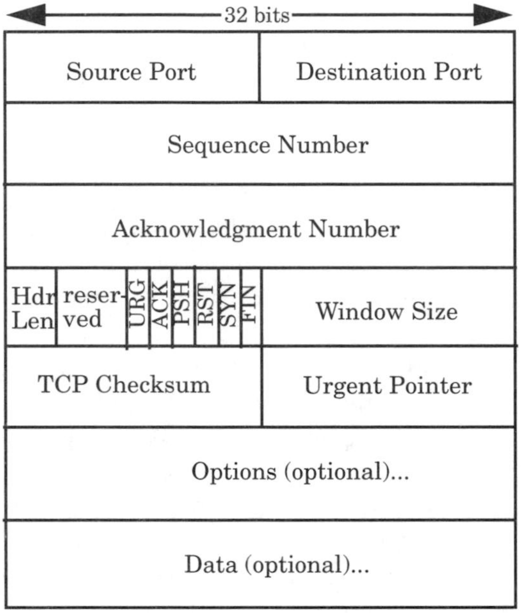

32 bits
Source Port
Destination Port
Sequence Number
Acknowledgment Number
Hdr Len
reser-ved
URG
ACK
PSH
RST
SYN
FIN
Window Size
TCP Checksum
Urgent Pointer
Options (optional)...
Data (optional)...

Figure 2-7. TCP header.

2.6.1 Segments, MSS, and MTU

When TCP receives data from the application, it breaks it into *segments*.

Each end of a connection can announce the Maximum Segment Size (MSS) it wishes to receive in an MSS option in the initial SYN packet. If no MSS is announced, 536 is used.[4] Larger values can be used, and may provide better performance since the per-packet cost of processing an IP header can be spread out over more data bytes [Mogul 1993].

The MSS can, of course, be no larger than the MTU of the local net, less headers, or fragmentation will occur immediately.

2.6.2 Sequence Numbers and ACKs

TCP uses sequence numbers to identify the location in a stream the data in the current segment goes. The receiver sends a segment with the ACK bit set back to indicate that it has received data up to (but not including) the byte identified by the number in the Acknowledgment Number field of the TCP header.

2.6.3 Ports

Each TCP connection not only connects two hosts, but also connects two *ports* on the hosts. The port is a way of allowing multiple connections to a single host. Usually a program on the host is associated with a given port. If a program waits for other programs to connect, it is often called a *server*, and the program that does the connecting is called a *client*, but the only real difference as far as TCP/IP is concerned is that one started the connection and the other accepted it. TCP connections are really between two peers, and any client/server or master/slave aspects of the relationship are arranged by consenting programs in the privacy of their own computers.

When a server starts up, it *listens* to a given port (if the port isn't already busy), which means that any connections made to that port will connect to the server.

When a program wishes to connect to the server, it looks up the "well-known port number" for the service, chooses a more-or-less random port for its own end of the connection and *connects* to the port on the remote host, thus establishing a connection to the server. See Table 2-2 for a sampling of well-known ports. The list is managed by the Internet Assigned Numbers Authority (IANA).

For example. imagine that we want to send mail to Fred at `fred@foo.example.com`. Our mail program collects our message, looks up the IP address of `foo.example.com`, chooses a local port and connects to `foo.example.com`'s mail transfer port, 25. Programs that listen on port 25 are expected to be mail servers.[5]

---

[4] 536 data bytes, plus 20 bytes of IP header and 20 bytes of TCP header, make a 576-byte packet; 576 was the MTU for the original ARPANET routers.

[5] Other "well-known" port numbers can be found in the latest "Assigned Numbers" RFC, which is RFC1700 as this is being written. On Unix hosts, these port numbers can usually be found in the file `/etc/services`.

Table 2-2. Well-known TCP ports.

Service Name	Port Number
echo	7
daytime	13
FTP	21
Telnet	23
SMTP (mail)	25
NNTP (Usenet news)	119
printer spooler	515
route	520

At this point, our mail program can use the standard SMTP mail protocol to specify the sender and receiver and then send our message across to the mail server on the other side, which will acknowledge receipt. Then we can close the connection, and the server will deliver the message to Fred.

(Error recovery, retrying failed connections, and all of the gritty details of mail have been cheerfully glossed over here with a great deal of vigorous hand-waving.)

The combination of the source and destination IP addresses and the source and destination ports fully identify a particular TCP connection. Note that this means that a given server (or client, for that matter) can have multiple connections to its port, since the IP address and port of the remote ends will all be different.

2.6.4 Connection Establishment

Figure 2-8 shows a complete picture of the TCP states. Each state is shown in an oval, and the allowed transitions are shown by the arrows. Each transition is labeled with the cause of the transition and the result. So where you see "rcv FIN/snd ACK," this means that when TCP receives a packet on this connection with the FIN flag bit set, the state of the connections is changed to the state at the other end of the arrow, and the action "send ACK" is done—a packet with the ACK flag bit set is then sent.

All connections are initially in the CLOSED state. Usually, CLOSED connections actually don't exist; when a connection is made they are created then.

To initiate a connection, one computer (usually called the client) does an *active open* by sending a packet with the SYN bit set and the initial sequence number. The connection moves to the SYN-SENT state.

The other computer, the server, which has previously performed a *passive open*, responds with a SYN packet containing the server's initial sequence number and an acknowledgment of the client's sequence number.

To complete the connection establishment, the client ACKs the server's initial sequence number. The connection is now *established*.

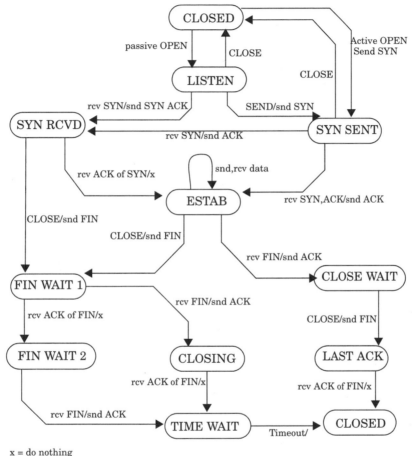

Figure 2-8. TCP state transition diagram.

On the server side, the server will do a *passive open* by listening on its assigned socket, and its connection stays in the LISTEN state until it receives the SYN from the client. It then sends back its own SYN and an ACK for the client's SYN, and then moves to the SYN RCVD state. When the client ACKs the server's SYN, the connection moves to ESTABlished.

2.6.5 Data Flow

Once the connection is established, the applications involved can send data back and forth. One side sends some data, the other side ACKs, the first side sends more, receiving ACKs until all the data are sent. The connection stays in the ESTAB state during the entire period of data flow.

TCP uses a *sliding window protocol* to control data flow. The window size field of the TCP packet tells the sender how much data the receiver is willing to accept. (This should be larger than the MTU or bad things can happen, as we'll see in Chapter 10.)

The sender will send a window's worth of data and then wait for the receiver to acknowledge the data. The receiver will send a packet with the sequence number of the last byte it received, and the sender will send more data.

If a packet is lost, the receiver will only ACK as much data as it has successfully received, and the sender will retransmit missing packets. If the receiver is receiving data faster than it can process it, it will send a smaller window, asking the sender to send less.

One of the keys to maximum performance (at least for bulk data transfer) is to manage the window so that the sender is sending continually and the link is kept busy. We'll see in Chapter 11 that this is not as simple as it looks.

2.6.6 Connection Termination

When either the client or the server wishes to terminate the connection, it sends a packet with the FIN bit set. The other computer must send back an ACK of this FIN, just as the SYN was ACKed in connection start-up. At this point, the connection is *half closed*.

Now, the other side can either continue to send data or more commonly it will also send a FIN, which the first computer ACKs. Now the connection is completely closed, and no further data can flow in either direction.

2.6.7 Other Header Flags

Several of the flags in the TCP header have not been described yet; they aren't really within the scope of this book, but for completeness I'll briefly describe them.

URG indicates that the *Urgent Pointer* in the header is valid; this means that the sender has put some "urgent data" in the data stream, and the "urgent pointer" contains a value to add to the sequence number to find the end of the urgent data. What the receiver does with this is not specified. It's used mainly for aborting transfers, such as typing the interrupt character in an rlogin session, or for killing off an FTP transfer.

PSH is the *push* flag. Mainly of historical interest, originally it was meant to be used to indicate that the data were to be sent as soon as possible, not waiting for buffers to fill or anything else.

RST is the *reset* flag. It is sent to terminate connections that are somehow improper. It is used when a connection request (a packet with SYN set) arrives, and no program is listening for connections on the port specified in the header. An attempt to connect to the WWW port on a machine not running a web server will trigger this. It's the server's way of telling the client "give up, no one is listening."

RST is also sent if a data packet arrives for a nonexistent connection. This can happen if a server crashes and reboots. The client will not be aware that the server has crashed and will keep retransmitting the last few packets according to the retransmission timeout algorithm. When the server comes back up far enough to initialize TCP/IP, it will receive these packets, recognize that there is no active connection for them, and send a RST to abort the connection. (Some TCP/IP stacks will time out connections after a certain amount of time; this is not specified in basic TCP/IP and is an extension).

2.7 User Datagram Protocol

In contrast to TCP, the User Datagram Protocol (UDP) is not a stream protocol. Whereas TCP hides (or at least, does not necessarily expose) the boundaries between packets, with UDP each output operation causes one UDP packet to be sent. There is no guarantee of delivery. Even so, UDP can be quite useful.

The format of a UDP packet (Figure 2-9) is quite simple. The first 32-bit word holds the source and destination port numbers, and the next holds the length and checksum. Using a 16-bit length means that the maximum length of a UDP packet is 65,535 bytes.

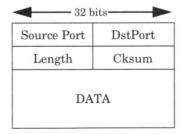

Figure 2-9. UDP packet format.

The UDP checksum covers the UDP header and data and provides some protection against data corruption. Some TCP/IP implementations have UDP checksum calculation disabled by default to improve performance, but this is a risky optimization. At a strictly local level, the Ethernet or other link-layer protocol provides CRC checking at the network frame level, but if the packet gets corrupted in some router between the source and destination, all that it guarantees is the correct transmission of an already corrupted packet.

2.8 Ethernet, Encapsulation, and ARP

A very common medium that TCP is used on is Ethernet. It's not directly relevant to ATM, but bear with me, as some of the problems encountered with putting IP on ATM are similar to those of putting IP on Ethernet, and we wouldn't want to forget history or we would have to do it over.[6] To transmit a packet on an Ethernet, an Ethernet header is placed at the front of the Ethernet packet (Figure 2-10).

Figure 2-10. Ethernet packet format.

The source and destination addresses are *Ethernet Addresses*, 6-byte numbers assigned to each Ethernet device by the manufacturer when built. Notice that these are not IP addresses. We know our own Ethernet address, since we can ask the Ethernet adapter in our computer for it, but if we want to send a packet to a given IP address, how do we determine the destination Ethernet address to put into the packet?

The answer is the Address Resolution Protocol (ARP) [Plummer 1982]. Using this protocol, we would broadcast a message on the network asking "who is IP address X, please tell me (Y)," and the host whose IP address is X should send back a message saying "I am X and my Ethernet address is Z." We now know X's Ethernet address and can send him packets directly. A refinement is to have all of the hosts on the net listen to "I am X and my Ethernet address is Z" messages in case they might want to send packets to X later.

2.9 Upper Protocol Layers

Above TCP and UDP are application protocols. Describing them in detail is beyond the scope of this book, but I will mention a few of the important ones to give a feel for why we're bothering with all of this.

---

[6] "We learn from history that we do not learn from history." —Georg Friedrich Wilhelm Hegel.

2.9.1 TCP-Based Protocols

A lot of the services that people think of when discussing the Internet are TCP-based. Here are descriptions of a few important protocols to give you the flavor of how these things work. Be warned that lots of details have been left out in the interest of saving space and getting on to the important (to this book) topics.

Telnet

Telnet is a protocol that allows a user on one computer to log in to another one connected to the same network and run commands on the remote machine. It was one of the earliest TCP/IP applications developed.

FTP

FTP stands for File Transfer Protocol and is used to transfer files back and forth over the network. The user's client program makes a TCP connection (called the control connection) to the server and then sends commands like

```
GET /pub/games/quake.exe
```

The server then makes a connection back to the client (called the data connection) to send the file.

The use of two connections—one for data and one for control—has the main benefit of making it easy to tell the difference between data packets and control messages. Anything arriving on the control connection at either the client or server must be a control message, and anything arriving on the data connection must be part of a file being sent.

Electronic mail

Electronic mail (e-mail) is carried over TCP in a text-based protocol called the Simple Mail Transport Protocol (SMTP) [RFC 822]. A typical SMTP session looks something like this (server responses in **boldface**, client requests are plain, my comments are in *italics*):

220 mail.baz.edu Esmtp;Sun, 20 Apr 1997 10:02:44 -0700
   The mail daemon announces its name and what time it is.
HELO example.com
250 mail.baz.edu Hello berry@example.com
   The sender tells the daemon who it is with the HELO command.
mail from: foo@example.com
250 foo@example.com... Sender ok
   The sender tells the daemon to whom it wants to send mail; the daemon
   replies with an indication that the address is probably OK.
RCPT to: joe@baz.edu
250 joe@baz.edu... Recipient ok
   The sender tells the daemon from whom this mail is coming.

```
DATA
```
354 Enter mail, end with "." on a line by itself
```
Hi Joe! Let's have lunch.
```
.

After the DATA command, the sender transmits the body of the message.
250 KAA02340 Message accepted for delivery
```
quit
```
221 mail@baz.edu closing connection
   All done; quit *closes the connection.*

Here the machine example.com connects to mail.baz.edu (using the well-known port for SMTP service). The server at baz.edu identifies itself, and example.com "logs in" with the HELO command. The next two requests identify who the mail is from and to whom it should be delivered. Then the body of the message is sent as DATA, and then we disconnect.

Notice that all of the server's responses are prefaced with a three-digit number. This is the "real" response code and is done this way so that it will be easy for the client code to figure out what happened without parsing the entire text message.

Luckily, Mail User Agents (MUAs)—the program you actually use to read your mail—and Mail Transfer Agents (MTAs), like sendmail or the POP server at your ISP, hide all of this protocol from the user; you'll never see it unless you get involved in implementing mail software, which is a relief.

Hypertext transfer protocol

Another TCP-based protocol is the Hypertext Transfer Protocol (HTTP), the infrastructure of the World Wide Web [RFC 2068]. It too is a text-based protocol. A WWW client or browser connects to a server and sends a request like

```
GET /x/y/z.html
```

and the server replies with the contents of the file z.html. The browser displays the file, the user clicks on a link, and another request is sent.

Text-based protocols like SMTP and HTTP are popular because they are easy to debug, and their operation can be checked out by using, say, Telnet to connect to the server. This is not always best from a performance point of view, though. An example that does not use text is the X Window System Protocol [Scheifler 1992]. Using X, a program called an X Server controls the display, keyboard, and mouse of a workstation, and client programs connect to it. The client programs get information about keystrokes and mouse clicks and ask the server to draw things on the screen. While X can be used over other networking systems, it is usually used over TCP.

2.9.2 UDP-Based Protocols

The main use of UDP is for the Network File System (NFS), first defined and implemented by Sun Microsystems [RFC 1094]. NFS is based on Sun RPC, a remote procedure call protocol.

The operating system kernel of the client machine is modified with a new NFS filesystem type, so that when a program tries to open, close, read, or write a remote file, the NFS code is called instead of the "normal" code for accessing physical disk drives. The NFS Filesystem code uses the Sun RPC protocol to communicate with the NFS server code running on the remote machine, reading and writing blocks of files on it.

Another widely used UDP-based protocol is the Simple Network Management Protocol (SNMP). This is widely used for remotely configuring and monitoring Internet network equipment (Section 7.2).

2.10 The Future of IP: IP Version 6

With the exponential growth of the Internet stressing the infrastructure quite hard, the IETF decided that it was time to revamp the venerable (in Internet years, at least) Internet Protocol. The new version of IP was called "IPng" for "IP, the Next Generation," while people were arguing over what it should be. Now that it's settled, it's being called IP Version Six, or IPv6 for short [RFC 1883].

IPv6 has a new packet format (See Figure 2-11) and is not directly compatible with IPv4, though plans exist to make the transition as easy as possible, and to ensure continued interoperation with the current IPv4 Internet. The "Next

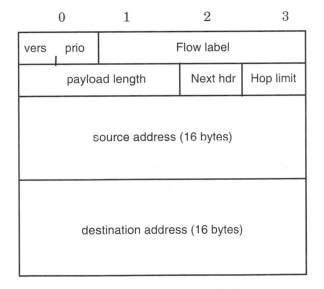

Figure 2-11. IPv6 packet header format.

hdr" field identifies the header type of the packet's data, exactly as the IPv4 proto field does.

2.10.1 128-bit Addresses

The address space of the current IPv4 Internet is rapidly being consumed, to the point where organizations with legitimate needs for large blocks of addresses are having a hard time obtaining them. In response, some rather odd schemes to hide "private" addresses behind some kind of address-translating gateway have been proposed [RFC 1631].

IPv6 addresses this problem with much larger 128-bit addresses. With a total number of 2^{128} or 3.4×10^{38} addresses available, address exhaustion ought not to occur again for a long, long time. Moreover, large addresses mean that hierarchical address assignment, formerly rejected as being wasteful, is practical after all [RFC 1887].

2.10.2 Dynamic Address Assignment

IPv6 has been designed to allow hosts to configure their IP address without a human being having to intervene. Just plug the IPv6 machine into the net, boot it up, and it will figure out its address "automagically."

Two mechanisms for doing this are provided. First, the machine can use the IPv6 version of the Dynamic Host Configuration Protocol (DHCP) to query a local DHCPv6 server for the needed information, or the machine can construct its address from the 48-bit MAC address of its interface card (MAC addresses are assigned by the card manufacturer and are supposed to be globally unique) and the 80-bit local subnet prefix it can learn from listening for packets from its neighbors.

2.10.3 Labeled Flows

The IPv6 packet header includes a new 24-bit field called the traffic-flow identifier. This should be useful for IPv6 quality of service (QoS) implementations, as the packets that belong to a connection for which a specific QoS was requested can be labeled with a unique identifier, allowing intermediate routers to make sure the proper QoS is maintained.

2.10.4 Multicast Support

IPv6 supports multicast traffic (see Chapter 8) in order to enable transmission of data (such as video or audio conferences, timely news, etc.) to widely dispersed hosts without needing global broadcast.

Besides mandating support for multicast as a basic part of the protocol, IPv6 introduces the notion of "anycast," whereby a host can transmit to an anycast address and get the data to a server—any server. Perhaps multiple redundant servers have been established to share a heavy load (as was done for the recent Mars Rover photographs). With anycast, a single address for the entire group of servers could be published and the load would be automatically directed to the "nearest" server.

2.10.5 Transition Plans

The transition from IPv4 to IPv6 has been carefully considered, the key being to maintain compatibility with existing IPv4 machines. [RFC1933] describes the mechanisms to be used by IPv6 machines that need to communicate with "legacy" IPv4 machines. Two mechanisms are proposed:

- supporting two independent IP layers, one for each of IPv4 and IPv6, useful for IPv6 hosts that must communicate directly with IPv4 hosts; and
- tunneling of IPv6 in IPv4 packets, useful for IPv6 hosts that must communicate across a network of existing IPv4 routers.

2.11 Summary

In this chapter we've seen how the Internet got started and how big it's grown. The basic operation of IP, ARP, and TCP were presented, and some of the typical services available with TCP/IP were described. We closed with a brief overview of IPv6.

Physical Media:
SONET and Others

One of the strengths of ATM is that it can use a variety of physical media, from twisted pairs of wires to optical fibers to radio links. In this section, I'll discuss how optical fibers function, and two of the most popular kinds of ATM links: SONET over optical fibers and Unshielded Twisted Pair (UTP).

3.1 Optical Fiber Communications

While several proposals for ATM over copper wires have been promulgated, optical fiber is still the most popular medium for ATM. Fiber-optic transmission offers long-distance transmissions and very low error rates. Fiber-optic cables are immune to electrical noise, since they are not electric! Also, since they carry no current, they can be installed in places where fire regulations don't allow copper wires.

Optical fibers transmit data by using modulated beams of light inside thin transparent fibers. Further, just about any networking technology that uses fibers can use the same fibers, so they are not likely to become obsolete soon. If you invest the considerable amount it takes to wire your building with fiber, you'll probably be able to use it for quite some time to come.

Optical fibers are constructed of a transparent core surrounded by an outside layer called cladding. These two parts of the fiber have differing indices of refraction, so that when light pulses are sent down the core, any light that tries to escape is directed back into the core by total internal reflection. (Just in case you don't remember this from freshman physics, here's a reminder.)

When light passes through an interface, such as that between air and glass, part of the light reflects and part refracts. Light reflects at the same angle as the incoming beam, but the refracted part is bent, the amount of bending depending on the *index of refraction* of the two media on either side of the interfaces (Figure 3-1). The amount of bending is described by Snell's Law

$$n \sin \theta = n' \sin \theta'$$

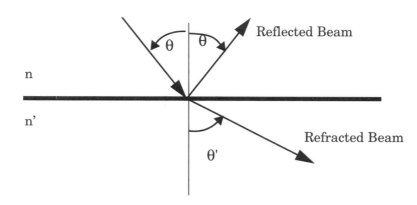

Figure 3-1. Refraction of light.

where n and n' are the indices of refraction of the materials that the light is passing through, and θ and θ' are the angles at which the light strikes and leaves the interface.

If the incoming light beam strikes the interface at an angle sufficiently small, and the ratio of the indices of the two media is sufficiently large, then the angle of the refracted beam goes to zero. *All* of the light is reflected back into the original medium. You've probably seen this when looking up from the bottom of a swimming pool: at a certain angle from the vertical you can no longer see *out* of the pool, just reflections of what's *in* the pool. This phenomenon can also be seen by looking through the side of a fish tank and up at the surface at a shallow angle.

So if we have a transparent fiber with a refractive index different from air and shine light in one end at a sufficiently shallow angle, the light just goes all the way to the far end, bouncing off the interface between the core and cladding like a ping-pong ball fired down a sewer pipe.[1]

   The cladding of an optical iiber is covered with various layers of jacketing materials to protect, strengthen, and support the fiber (Figure 3-2).

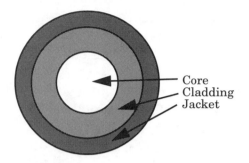

Figure 3-2. Optical fiber cross section.

   Fibers come in two flavors: single mode and multimode. Multimode fiber tends to have a larger core (typically around 50 μ) and suffers from *modal dispersion*: when light waves travel slightly different paths through the fiber, the pulses end up smeared at the far end. In Figure 3-3 we can see that one light beam takes a longer path than the other. A longer path takes more time to traverse, so the photons from a pulse inserted at one end emerge from the other at different times. The longer the fiber, the worse the smearing.

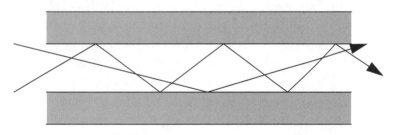

Figure 3-3. Modal dispersion in optical fibers.

   As we attempt to transmit more bits per second, raising the signaling speed, the pulses of light must become smaller in order to fit more in, and pulse smearing of modal dispersion becomes more and more of a problem.
   In single-mode fibers, the core is smaller (around 8 to 12 μ). Since this is closer to the wavelength of the light used, only a single path through the fiber "works"; "bad" paths cancel themselves out and modal dispersion is nearly eliminated. The fiber acts more as a waveguide. To accurately describe this phenome-

---

[1] This is the "particle model" of light; there is a wave model too but its metaphors aren't as much fun.

non requires using some advanced mathematics, but if you are curious check out [Green 1993] for a rigorous treatment of the subject.

Anyway, since single-mode fibers eliminate modal dispersion, higher signaling rates and longer transmissions paths are allowed, since the pulses of light are not smeared as much at the receiver end. (Another type of single-mode fiber uses a graduated refractive index to achieve the same effect.)

Multimode fiber is still widely used, despite single-mode fiber's advantages, because connections are easier to make with the fatter fibers, and the physical connectors are more tolerant of minor errors in assembly and alignment.

Optical transmitters can be based on either light-emitting diodes (LEDs) or semiconductor lasers. LEDs are cheaper, but lasers can emit more power in a narrower wavelength range and transmit longer distances. LED transmitters are typically used in local areas and lasers for long-distance Wide Area Network (WAN) applications.

3.2 Synchronous Optical Networking (SONET)

The SONET system was developed at Bellcore (once short for "Bell Communications Research" but now the official name of the company) at the behest of the Regional Bell Operating Companies (called RBOCs or sometimes "telcos" for "telephone companies") that were formed after the breakup of AT&T. It has since been incorporated into international standards by the ITU.

Because it is widely used for telecommunications backbones, SONET equipment is readily available. More important, SONET interface chips are seen as worth building by chip makers and can be used in computer equipment too!

The RBOCs desired a modern networking technology that would suit their needs for a long time to come. Specific desires were to have standardized, compatible equipment, so that companies could interconnect easily, to support Operations and Maintenance and Provisioning (OAM&P), allow efficient multiplexing, provide "survivable rings," and permit new services—like ATM.

The desire for compatible equipment standards is pretty obvious, at least to us Internet folks. If you hook up to the Internet, you want to be able to connect to any host. Public networks should be the same way. Customers don't want to have to sign up with multiple carriers to access all the places they want; they want to sign up with one carrier and let them worry about intersystem connections. With SONET as the standard, one can be pretty sure that just by connecting the fibers into the equipment, it ought to work.

OAM&P is the term for the low-level management built into SONET. As we'll see in Section 3.2.2, it allows fault detection and isolation and performance monitoring. "Provisioning" is the "telco" term for establishing new circuits.

One of the strengths of SONET is its multiplexing capabilities. Using devices called Add-Drop Multiplexers (ADMs), it is straightforward to add circuits the to SONET stream or drop them out at their destination.

SONET equipment is often configured in "rings" that allow automatic switching to alternate paths in order to survive failures. When you consider the revenue lost when a major phone trunk is cut, a little redundancy starts to look very attractive.

3.2.1 SONET Flavors

There are several confusing designations for standard transmission speeds.

Start with a single voice telephone line, a 64 kbit/sec ISDN B-channel, if you will. Carrying voice over a digital path requires that the analog sound of the caller's voice must be digitized, or converted, into a stream of numbers that represent the signal, rather like music for a compact disk. Now, telephone researchers have done a lot of work to figure out that most of the useful information in speech—the part that allows us to recognize and understand the human voice—lies below 4000 Hz or so. By compressing the dynamic range, that is, restricting the difference between the loudest and softest sounds, we can get the samples down to 8 bits or 1 byte each. Nyquist's theorem says that we need to sample at twice the highest frequency we wish to preserve, so we use 8 kHz as our sampling rate. Eight thousand 1-byte samples per second gives us 8000 byte/sec or 64,000 bit/sec.

Now let's take a look at the T1 line, which is designed to multiplex 24 voice channels. Since a voice line is 64 kbits, 24 of them gives 1.536 Mbits/sec. If we aggregate 32 of these T1s into another multiplexed unit, we get 49.152 Mbits. Adding some overhead for multiplexing, synchronizing, and maintenance information raises it to 51.84, the first *Synchronous Transport Signal* level, called STS-1.

The STS levels refer to the speed of the bitstream. When these bits are converted to a train of optical pulses in a fiber, they are called an *Optical Carrier*, or OC-1.

If we now multiplex three STS-1 lines together we get STS-3 at 155.84. The optical stream is called OC-3. You may see "OC-3c" referred to. This is simply the same bit rate as OC-3, but interpreted as one channel instead of three multiplexed OC-1s. The "c" stands for "concatenated," referring to the way the OC-1s are lumped together into one stream.

The CCITT (now ITU) had to get into the act and designated Synchronous Transport Module levels, starting with STM-1, which is approximately an OC-3. Table 3-1 summarizes the standard rates.

There are subtle differences between OC and STM standards, but they are not important here.

Table 3-1. SONET data rate designators.

Data Rate	SONET	CCITT
51.84	STS-1 OC-1	—
155.52	STS-3 OC-3	STM-1
622.08	STS-12 OC-12	STM-4
1244.16	STS-24 OC-24	STM-8
2488.32	STS-48 OC-48	STM-16

The bytes of data to be transmitted are packed into SONET frames as shown in Figure 3-4. Since SONET was originally conceived as a way to multiplex 64-kbit voice channels into larger packages, it is not surprising to see a hierarchical structure. The basic frame is 810 bytes arranged in nine rows and 90 columns. At STS-1 speed, one frame is sent at a time. (There are 8000 frames per second or one every 125 µs, which frequency derives from the 8 kHz voice sampling speed). For STS-3, three frames are sent at a time. Logically these frames are thought of as being sent in parallel, but in reality they appear sequentially on the fiber, just three times as fast as in an STS-1.

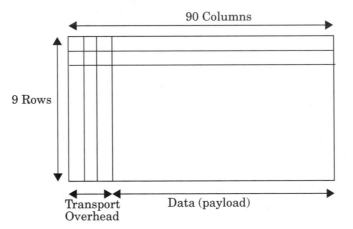

Figure 3-4. SONET frame structure (STS-1).

The first three columns of the frame are reserved for transport overhead. Astute readers with calculators readily at hand will notice that this implies that 27 out of the 810 bytes or 3.33 percent are reserved for overhead. Some of the overhead bytes are used for network management data, alarms, and maintenance voice channels. Other bytes are used for demultiplexing the data streams.

SONET gear includes regenerators, which simply repeat the bits they see, and Add/Drop Multiplexors, which can add bitstreams together (adding three OC-1s to make an OC-3, for instance) or tear them apart (stripping out the T3 that's destined to go down this fiber here, etc.)

SONET's designers worked carefully to make the system simple to maintain, at least for end users. At PARC, it is very easy to tell not only when the SONET links go down, but where the problem is. Maintenance costs for the public carriers are reduced too, with the result that some large customers are finding it cost-effective to replace multiple T3 connections with high-speed SONET links at less cost for more bandwidth.

3.2.2 Operations and Maintenance

One of the nicest things about ATM is the support for Operations and Maintenance (OAM). This feature allows some pretty neat diagnostics, monitoring, and more!

ATM's OAM is specified in the ITU-T Recommendation I.610. The components of OAM as set forth there include:

1. *Performance Monitoring*: You should be able to tell if your link is performing "as advertised." Is data being dropped somewhere?

2. *Defect and Failure Detection*: Any glitch or failure that affects data transfer should be monitored and reported automatically.

3. *System Protection*: These failures should not take down the whole net, and if something can be substituted to keep things going (a spare fiber already hooked up, for instance) use it! (This happened to us once: Through the good graces of Sprint we were using a spare fiber from Palo Alto to Kansas City for some experiments. A half hour before a big presentation, somewhere between here and there a backhoe severed a fiber carrying real, revenue-producing phone traffic and our "spare" fiber was suddenly no longer spare. Sprint's equipment switched the "real" traffic onto our "spare" fiber right away, the paying customers never noticed, but we panicked for about 15 minutes until a *spare* spare fiber was manually switched back in. The moral of the story (besides the telecom industry's love/hate relationship with backhoes, who bury the fiber when it's wanted as well as digging it up when it's not) is that this OAM feature prevented paying customers from being inconvenienced.)

4. *Defect Information*: When something bad happens you need to know who did what to whom or who's no longer doing what they should. OAM should report this.

5. *Fault Localization*: When you discover that something is wrong, you don't want a message like "Duh. The network's broken somewhere" (or even worse, just nothing happens for a long time). Fault localization

tells you instead that the link between Denver and Kansas City has
failed somewhere between the fourth and fifth regenerator, which puts
the fault just outside Wichita. Call out the helicopters to search for
backhoes!

OAM is defined to operate in a hierachical fashion. There are five levels as
shown in Figure 3-5. The first two are part of the ATM Layer, and the next three
belong to the Physical Layer.

- **F5: Virtual Channel Level**: the end-to-end connection between entities
  that terminate virtual channels. It extends through at least one Virtual
  Path.
- **F4: Virtual Path Level**: defined as the network between endpoints that
  terminate a Virtual Path. It extends through at least one transmission path.
- **F3: Transmission Path Level:** the network between elements that
  assemble and disassemble transmission system payloads. For SONET, this
  means boxes that multiplex SONET channels together. The transmission
  path traverses one or more digital sections. For ATM carried over SONET,
  this corresponds to the SONET Path layer.
- **F2: Digital Section Level:** corresponds to the SONET Line Level
- **F1: Regenerator Section Level:** applies over single-fiber runs, which can
  involve "regenerators" that receive, clean up, and retransmit the signals on
  long-haul links.

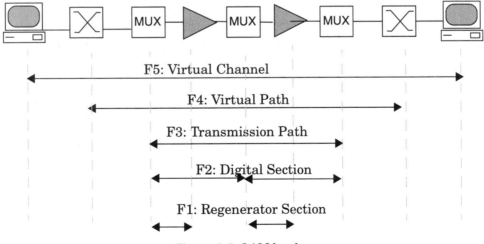

Figure 3-5 OAM levels.

OAM information is exchanged in the overhead section of the SONET
frames or in special ATM cells.

OAM Levels F4 and F5 are part of the ATM layer. These flows must be sent in ATM cells.

The F4 Virtual Path flow cells have the same VPI as the regular data cells being carried along the virtual path. Two types of data are carried in F4 flows: end-to-end and segment. The end-to-end flow is carried in cells with VCI=4, and the segment flow in cells with VCI=3.

The end-to-end flow carries information between entities that terminate a virtual path, while the segment flows operate along part of the path.

Here is a description of some the various alarms, signals, and indications that can occur, how they propagate and what they mean. I've tried to pare it down a bit from the complete list, which can be overwhelming, restricting it to those that a user or network manager will typically see. Here we begin to see what all that overhead in the SONET frame is good for.

Section signals

- **LOS:** Loss of Signal. This means that the receiver no longer sees light coming out of the fiber. Nothing is happening at all! This is detected at the lowest level (F1) and causes a Server Signal Defect at the SONET Line (F2) level.

- **LOF:** Loss of Frame. The SONET receiver cannot find valid SONET frames in the received bitstream. This is detected at the lowest level (F1) and causes a Server Signal Defect at the SONET Line (F2) level.

- **S-BIP:** Section-level Bit-Interleave-Parity error. A parity error was detected in a SONET frame at the Section level. No further signals occur; but the errors are usually counted.

Line signals

- **L-AIS:** Line-level Alarm Indication Signal. A downstream unit generated an alarm. This is detected at the Line (F2) level. A L-RDI is returned along the same path. (The unit is sending back a message saying "Hey! I saw an AIS from you.")

- **L-RDI:** Line Remote Defect Indication. An upstream unit saw a L-AIS whiz by. Detected at the Line level and counted.

- **L-BIP:** Line Bit-Interleave-Parity error. A parity error was detected at the Line level. A Far End Block Error (FEBE) is returned.

- **L-FEBE:** Line-level Far End Block error. An upstream unit detected a BIP at the line level.

Path-level signals

- **P-AIS:** Path-level Alarm Indication Signal. A downstream unit had an error and generated this AIS, causing an SSD.
- **P-LOP:** Path-level Loss of Pointer. The pointer indicates where in the SONET frame the data really start; if the pointer is nonsense, this error is generated. Causes an SSD to the next level.
- **P-BIP:** Path-level Bit Interleave Parity Error. A parity error was detected at the Path level. A P-FEBE is returned.
- **P-FEBE:** Path-level Far End Block Error. An upstream unit detected a BIP at the Path level.
- **Other Path Errors:** TIM: Trace Identifier Mismatch, SLM: Signal Label Mismatch, and UNEQ: Unequipped Signal all cause a P-RDI to be returned.
- **P-RDI:** An upstream unit detected one of the "other path errors."
- **LCD:** Loss of Cell Delineation. After decoding a SONET frame the receiver cannot tell where the cells are. Causes a SSD to the VP layer, as do the SSD's from the other Path level errors.

The AISs and some RDIs can be "spontaneously generated" by units detecting an error condition; the type of error is carried in the OAM cell in the appropriate flow. F1, F2, and F3 flows are not available at the ATM layer.

The F4 and F5 levels, or Virtual Path and Virtual Channel layers, each have AISs defined that trigger the sending of an RDI back downstream. Optionally, there may be continuity checking and performance monitoring implemented in the F4 and F5 flows, but not all equipment implements them.

3.2.3 Survivable Rings

A complete description of the myriad ways to configure SONET networks is a vast document indeed. One popular way is to configure a *self-healing ring* (Figure 3-6). These rings are often used for large public networks that must provide reliable service with minimal interruptions regardless of what calamity may befall any individual component.

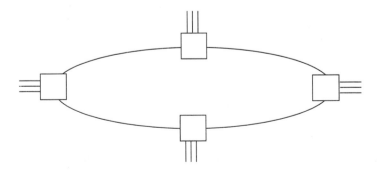

Figure 3-6. Self-healing ring.

Here are two ways to configure such a ring using redundant fibers and add-drop multiplexers:

1.   Unidirectional Path-Switched Ring (UPSR) and
2.   Two-Fiber Bidirectional Line-Switched Ring (BLSR) using two fibers.

The UPSR uses switching of subchannels at the SONET Path level, while the others switch at the Line level. While the ring itself makes a loop, usually subchannels are carved out of the loop bandwidth to provide point-to-point links for customers; the ring-ness allows these links to be rerouted in case of a failure.

Unidirectional path-switched ring

In the UPSR, the nodes are connected with a pair of fibers (Figure 3-7). One fiber in the pair is used as the working fiber, used to carry the traffic, and the other is the protection fiber, used in case of some kind of failure. From a given node, data entering the ring proceeds either clockwise or counterclockwise around the ring. At each node a path selector monitors the OAM flows to see if any faults have occurred. Although it is normally set to select the working ring, if a fault is detected, it switches to the protection ring, ensuring that data continue to flow in the face of any single failure.

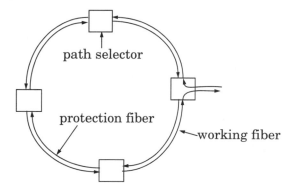

Figure 3-7. UPSR.

At first it appears that it would be a bad idea to lay both fibers in the same trench since a single backhoe stroke would sever both. It turns out to still work! Observe Figure 3-8. Data on the working fiber ring travels counterclockwise to node A as before. Nodes B and C can no longer receive cells this way, so when they receive the RDI indication or see the signal disappear altogether, they switch to receiving on the protection fiber, which already has a copy of the data stream. Transmissions from B and C reach other nodes just fine on the working fiber but node A's protection fiber has to carry its transmissions to the other node.

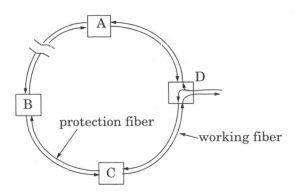

Figure 3-8. UPSR in failure mode.

Now, if we were to have *another* failure, things would break down, but this is a pretty good start at keeping things running in the face of failures.

Two-fiber bidirectional line-switched ring

A BLSR is similar in topology to a UPSR: Each node is connected to its neighbor with a pair of fibers. The difference is that traffic flows in *both* directions around the ring. Each fiber's bandwidth is divided into two parts, the working section and the protection section.

The advantage is that traffic between two nodes can flow along the shortest path between them, instead of being constrained to flow around the ring. For example, if we wish to provision a link between nodes A and B, we need two paths, one in each "direction." If we are using a UPSR, the data for one side go from A to B quite nicely, but data from B to A have to go around the ring the long way, since the ring is unidirectional (Figure 3-9).

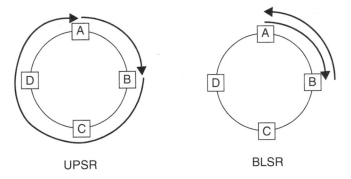

UPSR   BLSR

Figure 3-9. UPSR versus BLSR: bidirectional traffic.

Using the BLSR technique, each side of the link can follow the shortest path, reducing delay in the traffic and receiving nodes C and D of traffic they don't care about. This can lead to the ring handling more traffic than a UPSR, if the traffic is arranged properly.

Further, in addition to rerouting traffic in the event of a line failure, a BLSR can recover from a complete failure of a node.

3.3 Unshielded Twisted Pair

The other major physical medium used for ATM is copper wires in unshielded twisted pairs (UTP) [ATM Forum 1994a].

Copper wires have the advantage that they are less expensive than optical fibers, and techniques for working with wires are well understood, whereas optical fibers are still fairly new, and the tools for working with them are expensive.

The 155 Mbit ATM specification uses the standard SONET framing, so other than the final module that converts the SONET frame into bits on the cable, the rest of the hardware can be identical. In fact, some interfaces use daughter cards containing the physical medium interface, so that by swapping an optical fiber daughter card for a UTP one, a switch of the medium type is made whereas the rest of the board remains the same.

Twisted pairs are used to reduce interference with the signal from sources like radios, electric motors, and other computers, which can generate a lot of noise and swamp the good signal. The wires in our UTP cable act as antennas and pick up this noise, which generates currents in the wires. However, since the wires are twisted around each other, it is easily shown[2] that the currents in the two wires cancel each other out at each end.

Now, there's a limit to how much bandwidth can be stuffed into a copper wire. The exact amount depends on:

- the care with which the terminations are made,
- the uniformity of the twist in the cable,
- the electrical environment of the cable,
- the impedance of the connections, and
- the length of the cable.

Luckily, what is called "Category 5 UTP" cable is generally well made and entirely adequate for ATM over UTP. (Cat-3 is *not*, though!) The terminations must be made carefully, since if the wires are allowed to untwist even a little bit the shielding effect of the twist is lost.

The standard defines a "Reference Model" for UTP links that uses 90 m of backbone cable, 10 m of patch cords, and no more than four internal connectors.

---

[2] Whenever my Electricity and Magnetism prof used to say this I knew I was in for a heck of a problem set. *This* demonstration *is* fairly easy, though; consult any undergraduate E&M text for details. Yeah, I didn't want to go back and remember the math either.

In practice, as long as the attenuation limits for Cat-5 cable (as defined in EIA-568) are met, anything goes, but much more than 100 m of cable will get close to the performance limits.

ATM over UTP uses the same RJ-45 (or ISO/IEC 8877) connectors that ISDN and 10Base-T Ethernet do, but uses only two pairs from the cable.

3.4 Other Media

Other physical media can be used for ATM.

One of the first ATM media available was the 100 Mbit Transparent Asynchronous Transmitter/receiver Interface (TAXI). Early manufacturers and researchers used it because the TAXI chips were readily available since they are used in FDDI.

A lot of attention has been paid to 25 Mbit ATM over Category-3 UTP. The motivation is to provide better performance than Ethernet, but at lower cost than fiber or even 155 Mbit over Cat-5 UTP. Quite a few vendors ship products in this class, but some people think it's not such a good idea, arguing that 100 Mbit Ethernet is faster and cheaper; the 25 Mbit ATM proponents retort that at least they can interwork with their ATM networks directly. The bottom line seems to be that if a low cost ATM is needed, 25 Mbit ATM is OK, but if low cost and high speed are needed, and ATM interworking is not an issue, then 100 Mbit Ethernet with a switched hub may be a better choice.

There have even been implementations of ATM over links to satellites! For example:

- NASA Lewis Research Center has explored QoS parameters appropriate to satellite data links and the effect that varying link quality has on overall QoS.
- COMSAT Laboratories have developed transmission hardware to change the coding scheme in response to degradation of the satellite signal, enabling higher throughput in the face of poor reception.
- The SILAS project at the University of Aberdeen has done work on how to recover from noisy channels which corrupt the data, and how to deal with the long delays involved in sending data by way of a geosynchronous satellite.

3.5 Summary

In this chapter we learned how optical fibers transmit data. We saw how data are packed into SONET frames originally designed for carrying digital voice telephony, and some of the features that make SONET attractive, like scalability and survivability, were described. Finally, we looked at twisted pair cabling and briefly touched on some other media.

Asynchronous Transfer Mode

A bottom-up look at ATM technology

Now that we have seen how IP works and what SONET is, it's time to take a look at Asynchronous Transfer Mode itself. This chapter will look at it at a detailed but rather abstract level. We will leave the details of how to carry IP traffic over ATM for later chapters since there's more than one scheme.

4.1 Broadband Integrated Services Network

ATM is intended to be the low-level network technology to support the ITU's grand network of the future, the Broadband Integrated Services Network (B-ISDN). In the brave new B-ISDN world, this is supposed to supply data, voice, and other communications services over a common network, with a wide range of data speeds.

It must be remembered that ATM was designed by the telephone industry, working through the ITU, to meet their own needs for a better transmission technology and to allow new services.

The data networking community saw the technology that the ITU chose to build B-ISDN with and decided that it could work for them too, and the phone company could keep out of it!

Several factors combined to make the development of a new data-transfer technology attractive. For one thing, computing devices were getting faster. Modern personal computers rival the processor speed of mainframes of as little as ten years ago. Data transmission speeds keep getting faster too. Modems alone are pushing 56 kbits/sec, a speed only available through the best—and most expensive—leased lines when the ARPANET was built. Data transmission speed on trunk circuits is reaching into the gigabit range.

Furthermore, integrated circuit technology is improving. It enables very fast PCs and workstations and allows the construction of very fast network switching gear at continually shrinking costs.

Also, it is easier to build asynchronous equipment, where a transmitting station can send data at any time, than the traditional time-division multiplexing systems, where a transmitting station has to send in its time slice or wait for the next slice.

All of these factors, combined with a perception that current (at the time) protocols could not handle the foreseen high speeds made developing a new technology attractive.

4.2 B-ISDN Reference Model

To understand a lot of the terminology in ATM-land, it is necessary to understand the *B-ISDN Reference Model*. Just as the famous ISO Seven-Layer Model defined layers for network software, this model defines layers for the ATM network (Figure 4-1).

At the bottom is the *physical layer*, which deals with how the bits are encoded onto the wire or fiber. This layer will present a uniform interface to the upper ATM layer, but perform tasks specific to the physical medium being used. A SONET physical layer might keep track of SONET frames, error conditions, and alarms, and monitor the SONET OAM data. A physical layer concerned with TAXI fiber connections will have an entirely different set of concerns (which, considering the TAXI simplicity, could consist mainly of "Is there still a signal here?").

Next is the *ATM layer*, which deals with the formatting, sending, and relaying of cells.

Then comes the ATM Adaptation Layer (AAL), which maps Protocol Data Units (PDUs, or more commonly "packets") into cells in ways appropriate for the traffic.

The ATM AAL is subdivided into three parts or sublayers. The lowest level is the Segmentation and Reassembly (SAR) sublayer, which is responsible for segmentation, or receiving PDUs from the upper layers, shredding them into ATM cells, and sending them down to the ATM layer. It also performs reassem-

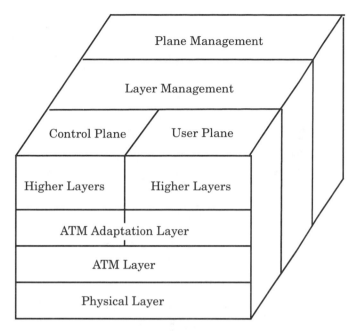

Figure 4-1. B-ISDN reference model.

bly; that is, receiving cells from the ATM layer and reconstructing the PDU from them and sending it to the upper layers.

The middle sublayer of the AAL is called the Common Part Convergence Sublayer (CPCS), and the top sublayer is called the Service Specific Convergence Sublayer (SSCS). The term "convergence sublayer" means that data streams from multiple applications may be funneling together here to be sent out onto the network, so they *converge* at this spot. The SSCS can be thought of as a "shim" layer to fit upper layer protocols to the AAL, and the CPCS performs functions common to all protocols. We will see examples when we discuss specific AALs later.

Finally, on top are all the higher layers of the protocol stack: IP, TCP, UDP, and so on.

However, there are also "planes," which are *vertical* slices through the protocol layer cake. The User Plane is what we are all used to dealing with: It manages the transfer of data to and from application programs. The Control Plane is new, however. It manages call establishment and release as well as other connection-oriented control functions.

Behind the U-Plane and C-Plane is the M-Plane: The Management Plane, which manages all this complexity.

In fact, most of the complexity here has little more substance than the ISO seven-layer model. Its main benefit is for discussing design issues; the conceptual separation of control and user data flows is useful, for instance.

4.3 ATM Concepts

4.3.1 What's Asynchronous About It?

One of the first questions people ask about ATM is "What's asynchronous about it?" It's a good question.

A fundamental technique in data communications is the multiplexing of many streams of data over a single physical link. There have been many different techniques invented to solve this problem.

Some systems assign each sender a time slot during which it can transmit data. ATM does not do this; an ATM device can transmit whenever a cell is ready. The cells themselves are sent *synchronously* over the SONET link, but each station can *asynchronously* send as many or as few cells as it needs to, whenever convenient (subject to bandwidth reservation policies).

4.3.2 Hierarchical Network Structure

ATM networks are organized in a hierarchical fashion (Figure 4-2), rather like current telephone networks, which is hardly surprising. In the usual view, ATM end stations are connected to private networks through a User-Network Interface (UNI). Networks themselves are connected to each other by Network Node Interfaces (NNIs).

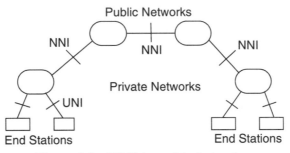

Figure 4-2. ATM hierarchical structure.

The UNI used usually depends on whether ATM end stations are being used in a public or private network. Private networks tend to use the ATM Forum defined UNI 3.1, while public networks use ITU-T's Q.2931. They are quite similar.

What happened was that the ITU extended the existing Q.931 ISDN signaling standard to include variable bandwidth and quality of service features, and produced Q.93B. The ATM Forum then added point-to-multipoint connection support and produced their specification UNI 3.0. Next, the ITU decided to align their standard with the ATM Forum's specification, but did a few things differently, resulting in Q.2931. Finally the ATM Forum, wishing to make the different proposals interoperate, produced a close alignment in UNI 3.1.

The latest result from the ATM Forum is UNI 4.0, which adds support for switched virtual paths and receiver-initiated joins to multipoint circuits.

4.3.3 Cells

ATM uses small fixed-size packets called *cells*. Using cells has a few advantages. It allows for more efficient hardware design. It's easier to design a packet processor if you know in advance that packets will always be the same size. In fact, given that a cell is 53 bytes or 265 bits, it's not inconceivable that one could build a device with a cell bus that is that wide, so that a cell could be transferred in one clock cycle.

Another feature of using small cells is that head-of-line blocking is eliminated. This is a nasty phenomenon that occurs when high-priority data is delayed because large but low-priority packets have tied up a resource. Figure 4-3 shows that even though packet A arrives at the switch soon after the beginning of packet B, it still has to wait for packet B to be completely transmitted before it can be sent.

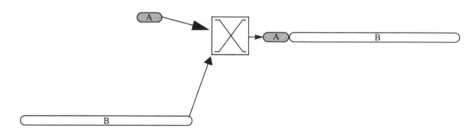

Figure 4-3. Head-of-line blocking.

On the other hand, if the packets are broken up into small cells, packet A can be sent between two of packet B's pieces (Figure 4-4). Thus high priority, delay-sensitive traffic can be interleaved with pieces of a low-priority bulk data transfer. That way, someone downloading the beta-software-du-jour won't delay packets of the boss's important voice conference[1] negotiating next-round funding with the venture capitalists.

---

[1] It is interesting and perhaps counterintuitive that voice (and sound in general) turns out to be *more* sensitive to dropouts and delays than even video. Drop a packet from a video stream and our eyes and brain smooth over the glitch, but drop or delay a voice sample and the glitch sounds *terrible*!

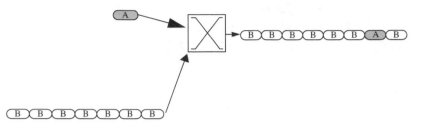

Figure 4-4. Head-of-line blocking eliminated.

4.3.4 Connection-Oriented

One of the most important aspects of ATM for someone coming from the IP viewpoint is its connection-oriented nature. Whereas in IP a host sends a packet into the network and "hopes" it arrives at its destination, with ATM, a connection must be set up between endpoints before any data can flow. This means that it can take longer to get a connection set up, but on the other hand, once it is, you can be pretty sure the data will continue to get there. In addition, IP might reroute your packets when a link goes down, but when an ATM connection dies, you are basically stuck with a dead connection.

4.4 What Cells Look Like

The compromise cell size decided by the CCITT for ATM was 53 bytes: 5 bytes of header and 48 bytes of "payload" or data (Figure 4-5). An ATM cell is formatted as shown in Figure 4-6.

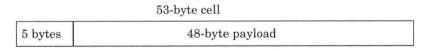

Figure 4-5. ATM cell format.

The meanings of the fields of the cell are as follows:

- **GFC**: Generic Flow Control
- **VPI**: Virtual Path Identifier
- **VCI**: Virtual Circuit Identifier
- **PTI**: Payload Type Indicator
- **CLP**: Cell Loss Priority
- **HEC**: Header Error Check
- **Payload**: The Data

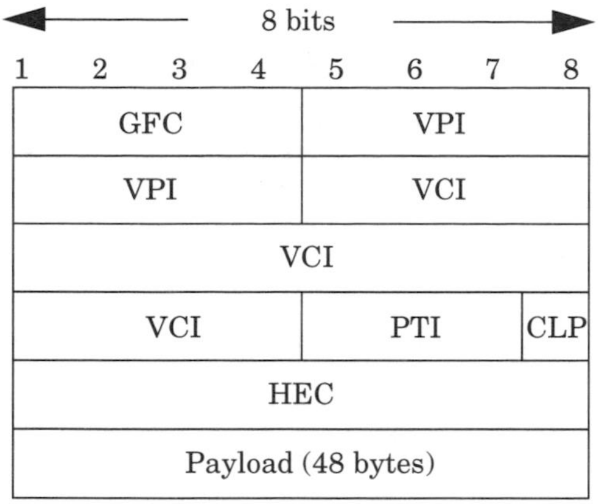

Figure 4-6. ATM cell header format.

Generic Flow Control is only used locally for various functions; its use is not yet standardized. Public Switches will set this field to zeros.

The Virtual Path and Virtual Channel Identifiers are used for routing cells inside the switch and from switch to switch.

The Payload Type field is used to indicate whether the payload in this cell is "user information" or control information. (It is also used by AAL5 to indicate end of frame; see Section 4.7.4.)

The Cell Loss Priority bit can be used to mark cells that should be discarded first if congestion occurs; a typical use would be if a host sends more cells than it is allowed by its bandwidth reservation.

The Header Error Control is an 8-bit CRC calculated over the header only. It can be used to detect multiple bit errors and to correct single bit errors. (Most equipment just detects all bit errors and flushes the cell.)

4.5 Switches

A central part of the ATM system is the switch. The switch is conceptually very simple: it has input ports, a VCI mapping facility, a switching fabric and output ports (Figure 4-7).

When a cell comes in to an input port, the switch looks at the VPI and VCI fields in the cell header and consults a table to determine the output port it should go to. It then rewrites the header of the cell to have the new VCI for the next hop and finally arranges for the cell to be routed to that output port by the switching fabric.

Each input and output port may have buffers or queues that can hold a number of cells. How large these buffers should be depends on the kind of traffic expected and is a matter of no little controversy. If regular, predictable loads are

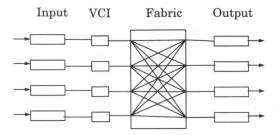

Figure 4-7. Typical generic switch.

expected, then small input buffers of a few dozen cells will suffice. If bursty traffic is expected—and Internet traffic tends to be extremely bursty—then large buffers may be needed to allow for momentary congestion and to provide time for rate control feedback to reach the sender.

Imagine two cells arriving simultaneously on two of the input ports of our generic ports and that they need to be sent to the same output port. Most switch designers agree that simply throwing away one of the cells is a, shall we say, suboptimal strategy.[2] If the links are not being run at full speed, then there is plenty of unused time to send the extra cell if we can just arrange for it to be saved somewhere until it's time for the next batch of cells to flow through the switch fabric.

There are two places to buffer the cells that cannot make it through the switch—the input port and the output port. (There are other schemes, such as the internally buffered Benes network, but they tend not to be in widespread use.)

With output buffering, the output port must be able to accept cells from all the inputs at once and hold them. If we could give each output port infinite memory for these buffers, then we could be sure that we would never drop a cell. Since infinite memory tends to be expensive, the switch designer has to decide how to balance the cost of the buffers with the probability that a cell would be dropped. Luckily for us poor folks who have to buy the switches, mathematical analysis of the problem indicates that relatively modest queueing at the output ports will deal with the vast majority of the problem (assuming the traffic follows certain arrival patterns).

With input buffering, we need some way of being able to answer the question "If I launch this cell into the switch fabric now, will it make it out the other side?" If the answer is no, then hold the cell until the next cycle. There are several difficulties here; some obvious ones are:

- the need to have the fabric and output ports send the data back,
- the fact that unless things are implemented carefully, one data stream could be starved out altogether while another stream flows merrily on through.

---

[2] This is research-speak for "This strategy is *terrible*! Only an *idiot* would do it that way!" But researchers who actually talk this way don't get more funding.

- While a cell is held up waiting for the output port to free up, another cell in the same input port that can go through is also held up—another form of Head-of-Line Blocking.

Many schemes have been thought up to deal with these (and other) problems but are beyond our scope. Suffice it to say that switch designers are clever folks. A few switches have both input and output buffering, allowing very good performance with quite a bit of resiliency to bursty traffic.

4.6 Virtual Circuits

The term *virtual circuit* is used to designate a pathway through a switch or switches to a destination machine. The virtual circuit identifier (VCI) is a number used to represent the circuit. It is important to realize that this number has no relation to the network addresses of the systems involved, the port addresses on the switch, or any other address. Consider your telephone: The ID number the phone company assigns to the pair of wires that comes to your house bears no relation to your actual phone number. Furthermore, once you call someone and establish a circuit with them, the ID number on their phone wires bears no relation to the ID on yours. In fact, you probably don't even know—or *need* to know—the circuit ID on your phone cable.

The telephone analogy is not accidental, by the way; remember that ATM was developed by folks who wanted a better ISDN.

Virtual paths are used to route groups of virtual circuits between switches. A switch routing cells based on a virtual path will send them all to the destination port designated for that path without looking at the VCIs; they get decoded later at another switch.

Permanent virtual circuits (PVCs) are currently widely used in local area ATM networks. They are set up by hand to connect systems and are therefore useful but cumbersome. Further, in "large" networks they can rapidly overwhelm the switch VCI routing memories. (Imagine if you had to have a wire connected to every phone on the city, just in case you wanted to talk to someone!) Therefore, switched virtual circuits (SVCs) are to be preferred seeing that each connection is established as needed and torn down when finished. This requires more sophisticated software to manage the connections, as we will see later.

4.7 ATM Adaptation Layers

4.7.1 What Is An AAL?

There must be a mapping from the data on the user level into the cell stream. This is the job of the ATM Adaptation Layers (AALs).

Each AAL is divided into two parts:

1. the segmentation and reassembly (SAR) sublayer, which distributes the data into cells and reassembles the data stream at the receiver and

2. the convergence sublayer, which manages the flow of data to and from the SAR sublayer.

There are four AALs defined by the ITU:

*   **AAL1**: used for constant bit rate services with maximum allowed delay requirements, such as video,
*   **AAL2**: used for variable bit rate services that also have delay requirements,
*   **AAL3/4**: used for data, and
*   **AAL5**: also used for data.

Historically, AALs 3 and 4 turned out to be so close that they were merged into AAL3/4. However, due to its complexity and poor interaction with computer hardware architectures, it was not very popular, and a much simpler AAL was standardized as AAL5.

4.7.2 AAL1

The purpose of AAL1 is to provide transport of constant bit-rate traffic through the ATM network and ensure that it arrives at its destination with the same constant bit rate.

AAL1 uses one byte at the beginning of each cell's payload to provide some SAR information. The byte is divided into two 4-bit segments called the sequence number (SN) field and the sequence number protection (SNP) field (Figure 4-8).

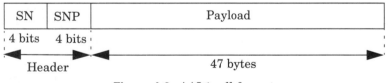

Figure 4-8. AAL1 cell format.

The first bit of the SN field is used by the convergence sublayer to signal "service-specific" data. Usually, this is something such as the beginning of a block of data. The next three bits are a sequence counter to detect dropped cells.

The SNP field "protects" the sequence number field by holding a 3-bit CRC over the SN field. The last bit of the SNP is chosen to ensure even parity over the first byte of the cell.

4.7.3 AAL3/4

AAL3/4 is the result of merging AAL3 and AAL4. It is widely considered too cumbersome and inefficient for data communications purposes and has been mostly replaced with AAL5. I'll describe it anyway, for historical interest, to show how cumbersome it really is, and because it is not completely dead yet.

To encode a datagram with AAL3/4, first it must be wrapped in the convergence layer header and trailer (Figure 4-9).

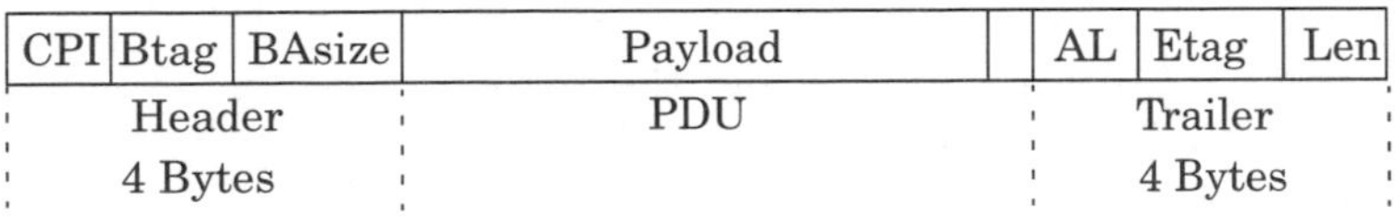

CPI	Btag	BAsize	Payload		AL	Etag	Len
	Header		PDU			Trailer	
	4 Bytes					4 Bytes	

Figure 4-9. AAL 3/4 PDU format.

The header is four bytes and consists of three parts. The Common Part Indicator (CPI) is 1 byte and is supposed to allow different header and trailer interpretations. Only one is defined, so this field is always set to 0, which means that the BAsize and Length fields are encoded as an integer number of bytes. The BAsize field is 2 bytes, and indicates the size of the buffer needed to store this packet, so the receiver can allocate the buffer when it gets the first cell (containing this header). Note that using 2 bytes for the BAsize field means that the maximum size of the payload is $2^{16} - 1$ bytes, or 65,535. The BAsize field can be larger than the length of the PDU, if it is thought that additional buffering might be necessary, so it cannot be assumed that the length of the PDU is the same as the BAsize field.

Btag and Etag are each 1 byte and are used to ensure that the header and trailer of a received packet do in fact belong the same packet and are not from different packets, somehow damaged and concatenated by a network problem.

The Payload field is padded to make sure that the trailer is 32-bit-aligned. (That means 0 to 3 bytes. The padding is the empty box to the right of the payload) and the AL field is simply to make sure that the trailer is 4 bytes long. Why they didn't just specify 1 to 4 bytes of padding is not clear to me. Perhaps having the trailer the same length as the header was important for symmetry or something.

The Length field encodes the length of the PDU, exclusive of the padding, header, and trailer.

Next, having wrapped the data in this encapsulation, the resulting packet is cut into 44-byte chunks and stuffed into cells. Each cell is also formatted with a header and trailer (Figure 4-10). The 2-bit T field indicates the type of cell: beginning, middle, or end of message, or if the PDU was small enough, a single-cell message. The 4-bit SEQ sequence number counts cells in the packet (modulo

16). The 10-bit MID multiplexing identifier is supposed to allow multiplexing cells on a single virtual circuit; it is little used and widely debated.

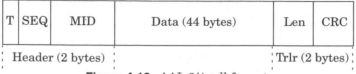

Figure 4-10. AAL 3/4 cell format.

The Len field is 6 bits and counts the bytes in the data field of the cell, which is always 44, unless the cell is the last of a packet. (If the cell is a single-cell packet, it is the first *and* the last cell of the packet at the same time.)

Notice that the 44 bytes of data per cell is not 32-bit aligned. This means that if you are writing code to implement AAL3/4[3] you either need to do some 2-byte transfers instead of all longword transfers, slowing down the code, or offset the cell, so that you can fill it in with longword transfers, but then the code that sends it out to the physical layer has to do the short transfers. Some clever hardware can help here; one early ATM host adapter, the FORE ASX-100, had cleverly designed registers that could be written in a set of longword transfers, but the first one had 2 bytes as "don't cares." This was great for software implementations of AAL3/4 but meant that software AAL5 was more complicated than it needed to be.[4]

The 10-bit CRC field is calculated over the whole cell.

To summarize, to send a packet using AAL3/4 the following steps take place (Figure 4-11).

First, the packet to be sent is padded to a multiple of 4 bytes. Next, the packet-level header and trailer are added, filling in the BAsize and LEN fields and choosing an appropriate tag for the Btag and Etag fields.

Then this wrapped packet is sliced into 44-byte chunks, and each chunk is wrapped in its own header and trailer, with the appropriate SEQ, MID, LEN, and CRC fields. LEN at this level is always 44, unless the last slice of packet doesn't fill the last cell.

Finally, the ATM cell headers are put on each wrapped chunk, and the cells are sent on the appropriate virtual circuit.

When the cells are received, one way to recover the packet would be this:

Check CRC's on received AAL3/4 cells. When a cell with the T field indicates that it is the beginning of a packet, extract the BAsize from the header (contained in this first cell) and allocate a buffer of that size for the packet.

---

[3] With Verilog and VHDL so popular, a lot of hardware design these days *is* writing code.

[4] To be fair, this board was designed while AAL5 was still being argued about in the standards committees so we can't expect the designer to have optimized the hardware for it.

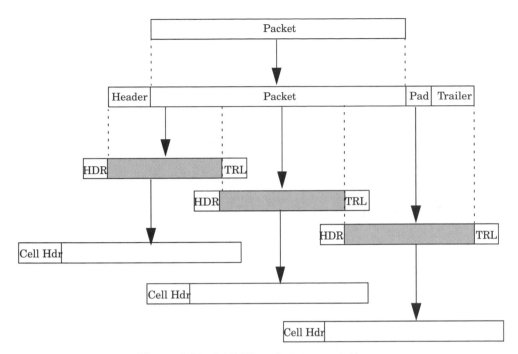

Figure 4-11. AAL3/4 packet segmentation.

Check SEQ and LEN and copy that many bytes to the buffer. When the cell with T indicates end-of-message, copy LEN bytes, extract the trailer from the cell, check that the overall packet length matches the value in the trailer, and pass the reassembled packet to the appropriate higher-level protocol.

4.7.4 AAL5

AAL5 was developed as a response to AAL3/4's complexity. It seemed that AAL3/4 had been deliberately designed to make efficient implementations impossible. AAL5 (known for a while as the Simple and Efficient Adaptation Layer [SEAL]) was designed to have less overhead, be capable of efficient implementation, and behave like existing datacommunications interfaces.

The data to be sent are padded and an 8-byte trailer added (Figure 4-12). The padding is calculated so that the data, pad, and trailer will evenly fill a number of cells. The trailer has two unused 1-byte fields, a 2-byte length (indicating the length of the data, not including the trailer and pad), and a 4-byte CRC (identical to the Ethernet CRC32 [Hammond 75]).

After the PDU is padded and trailered, it is simply chopped up into 48-byte chunks and sent in ATM cells.

The PTI field in the cell header is used to indicate the last cell of a packet. This allows a receiver to simply accumulate cells until it gets the last one, check

Payload		Pad	UU	CPI	Len	CRC
				Trailer (8 bytes)		

Figure 4-12. AAL5 PDU format.

the length and CRC, and pass the data on. In fact, it has been shown that this AAL is as good as AAL3/4 at detecting errors.

AAL5 is less wasteful than AAL3/4, since all 48 bytes of every cell except the last one are used for data. AAL3/4 by contrast takes 4 bytes out of 48 for overhead (an 8.3 percent overhead on top of the unavoidable 5 bytes out of 53 or 9.43 percent that ATM cell structure imposes).

4.8 Addresses

Just as computers on an Ethernet need Ethernet addresses, computers that operate on ATM networks need ATM addresses (Figure 4-13). There are several formats for ATM addresses promulgated by various standards bodies, but they all are 20 bytes long, which are a lot of addresses. At 160 bits, there's enough space for 1.46×10^{48} separate addresses. For comparison, the mass of the Earth is about 5.97×10^{27} gm, and the Sun's mass is 1.98×10^{33} gm. This means if we were uniformly assigning addresses to the Sun, each gram of the Sun could have as many as 7.4×10^{11} or 740 billion addresses.

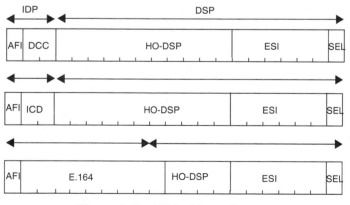

Figure 4-13. ATM address formats.

Now that's a lot of addresses, and I've proved I can use my calculator, but so what? The point is not how many addresses can dance on the head of a pin, but that having such a large address space to play in allows us to use hierarchical or structured address assignment and still have plenty of space left in the address.

So in true hierarchal style, the first byte of an ATM address is always the Authority and Format Identifier (AFI), which governs how the rest of the address is to be interpreted. Choices include DCC ATM Format, ICD ATM Format, and E.164 Format.

The AFI is the first part of the Initial Domain Part (IDP). What the IDP looks like depends on the AFI, of course. Following the IDP comes the Domain Specific Part (DSP) (Table 4-1).

Table 4-1. ATM Address Acronyms and Abbreviations.

Acronym	Meaning
IDP	Initial Domain Part
DSP	Domain Specific Part
AFI	Authority and Format Identifier
DCC	Data Country Code
ICD	International Code Designator
HO-DSP	High-Order DSP
ESI	End Station Identifier
E.164	ITU Recommendation
SEL	Selector

DCC addresses use the Data Country Code format. The 2-byte DCC field identifies the country the address is registered in, using codes specified by ISO. DCC addresses are assigned by countries.

ICD Addresses are used by International Organizations. The 2-byte International Code Designator identifies the organization.

E.164 addresses use the address format designed for ISDN. A "telephone number" up to 15 digits long is coded in a 9-byte BCD[5] field.

The Domain Specific Part (DSP) is interpreted according to the rules of the domain. Using DCC addresses, for example, every country can have its own way of interpreting ATM addresses. Luckily it is not that anarchic. The DSP is divided into two parts. First comes the High-Order DSP, which varies in length according to the address format. The authority issuing the address can use this part to encode routing topology, or hierachical structure, or whatever makes sense.

---

[5] BCD = binary-coded decimal; two decimal digits are packed per byte, so 1234 coded in BCD and notated in hexadecimal looks like 0x12 34.

The second part of the DSP consists of the 6-byte End Station Identifier (ESI) and a 1-byte Selector (SEL). The ESI/SEL are present in all ATM addresses. The ESI can be filled with a unique IEEE low-level Media Access Control (MAC) (or "Ethernet"-style) address. Since the MAC addresses are supposed to be globally unique, we wind up with a part of the address that stays with the end station (and unambiguously identifies it) and the rest of the address (that can change if the machine is moved around in the network) and describes (in a possibly convoluted way) how to get to it.

If you are setting up an ATM network that you expect to be completely private to your organization and will never connect to a public ATM network, you can pick any address scheme you like. If you expect to do signaling with a public network, though, you will have to coordinate with it on what address range to use.

4.9 Signaling

Signaling is the technique whereby virtual circuit connections are made on demand and discarded when they are no longer needed. The relevant standard for local networking is the ATM Forum's UNI 3.1 document.

Signaling is analogous to what happens when you dial a phone number, requesting a connection to another phone, and the phone company equipment decides which wires your call will go over. In fact, ATM signaling is based on telephone signaling algorithms and standards. The terminology is very similar; making a network connection is called "making a call" and so on.

4.9.1 SAAL and SSCOP

In order to send signaling messages, the switches and end stations need to agree on a protocol for carrying these messages. The protocol specified for this purpose is called the Service-Specific Connection Oriented Protocol (SSCOP). This protocol lives between the actual signaling code and the ATM layer and provides reliable transport of data (Figure 4-14).

SSCOP is based on the receiver granting "credit" to the sender, which then sends packets until it runs out of them; when the receiver is ready to accept more data it sends another "credit" packet to the sender.

It is a fairly complicated protocol and really only worth discussing if you are implementing ATM signaling code, in which case consult ITU recommendation Q.2110.

Signaling messages are sent by convention over the virtual circuit with VPI=0, VCI=5. AAL5 is used by SSCOP to map its packets into cells and back again.

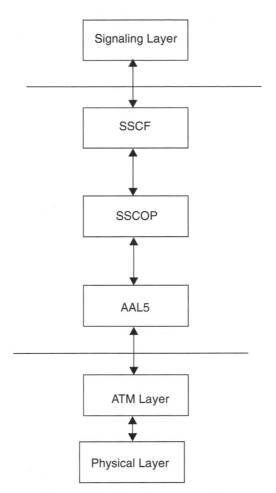

Figure 4-14. Signaling protocol layers.

4.9.2 Signaling Messages

Signaling messages are sent between nodes in order to carry out signaling functions. The messages of interest to us[6] are:

- **SETUP**
- **CALL PROCEEDING**
- **CONNECT**
- **CONNECT ACKNOWLEDGE**
- **RELEASE**
- **RELEASE ACKNOWLEDGE**

---

[6] Details are in the UNI 3.1 document [ATM FORUM 93].

The messages are encoded in a standard way (Figure 4-15). A 9-octet header is followed by a list of *Information Elements*, each coded in the same way (Figure 4-16).

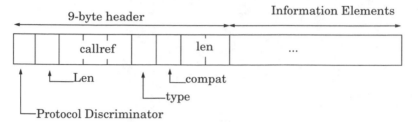

Figure 4-15. Signaling message format.

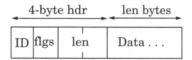

Figure 4-16. Information element coding.

Message header

The header contains the Protocol Discriminator, a value that identifies the message as a UNI Signaling message. It is coded as the value "5". Other values are reserved for other signaling messages, "National use," or other network layer protocols.

The next item in the header is the *call reference*. This is used by the end station making the request and by the switch to identify which call the message applies to. This allows multiple calls to be in progress at once.

First there is 1 byte with the length of the call reference value, which is always 3 under UNI3.1. Then comes the call reference value itself, making a total of 4 bytes.

The most significant bit of the 3-byte call reference value is used as a flag. This call reference flag is set to 0 if the sender originated the call and to 1 otherwise.

A value of 0 for the call reference is called the *global call reference*; it is used when it is desired to affect all active call references on a given channel.

Continuing our tour through the message header, we come next to the *message type* field. We find 1 byte that identifies what kind of message this is: SETUP, RELEASE, and so on, followed by another byte with a 1-bit *flag* and a 2-bit *action indicator*. For UNI3.1, these should be coded as 0, effectively ignoring them, but in the full glory of Q.2931, the flag indicates if normal error processing should occur, or if set, that if an error occurs, the action specified should be performed. Possible actions are "clear call," "discard and ignore message," or "discard and report status." The fourth possibility (2 bits have four values) is reserved.

Finally, the last field of the header is the *message length*. It is 2 bytes long and holds the length of the rest of the message, that is, excluding the header.

Information elements

The rest of the information in a signaling message is encoded in variable-length information elements, sometimes called IEs. These always start with a header as seen in Figure 4-16, which allows entities that do not actually "understand" a given information element to at least skip over it. A switch that does not support Quality of Service (QoS) features might still get requests with QoS specifications; stylized coding of the elements allows it to skip what it cannot process.

The first byte tells us what kind of information element this is: Address, call state, AAL parameters, etc.

In the next byte, 2 bits are used for flags. They identify the coding standard used in the information element: whether to use ITU coding or whatever is present in the network.

The rest of the byte is the *IE instruction field*, which instructs us what to do if there is an error while processing the information element. There's a flag bit to tell whether to pay attention to the IE Action Indicator or not and the Action Indicator itself. There are 3 bits worth of action possibilities here: Clear call, discard IE and proceed, discard IE and proceed and report status, discard message and ignore, and discard message and report status. (The other three possibilities are reserved.)

Next comes the 2-byte length field, and finally the information element data follows.

Following the IE data is the next information element, until as many bytes as specified in the message header have been consumed.

This style of coding information elements is sometimes called type-length-value (TLV), since that is the essence of the three fields involved.

SETUP message

We'll look at one message in detail as an example and summarize the rest.

The SETUP message has the information elements, shown in Table 4-2. Together with things that would be expected, like the calling and called party numbers (Sounds like a phone call, doesn't it? That's not an accident.) are items that identify:

- Which AAL is to be used for this connection?
- What is the traffic on this connection expected to be like? If we are requesting too much, the network may decide to reject the call; if we ask for

too little, we may not get all of our cells through. Like Goldilocks, this allows us to ask for bandwidth that's "just right."

- What QoS do we need? Are we willing to pay for expensive low-delay, guaranteed delivery, or will it be sufficient if we are allocated cheaper, "leftover" bandwidth?
- Which network should be used to carry this traffic? In the grand scheme, a user can pick the transit network just as a person can (at least in the U.S.) select a carrier for long-distance phone calls by dialing a special code. The Transit Network Selection information element carries the "long distance carrier" selection.

Table 4-2. SETUP message information elements.

Information Element	Size	Description
AAL parameters	4–21	Identify AAL
ATM traffic descriptor	12–30	Describe traffic parameters
Broadband bearer capability	6–7	Select bearer service
Broadband high layer info.	4–13	Higher layer characteristics
Broadband repeat ind.	4–5	Repeat next IE
Broadband low-layer information	4–17	Lower layer characteristics
Called party number	< 25	ATM address to connect to
Called party subaddress	4–25	ATM subaddress
Calling party number	< 25	ATM address connecting from
Calling party subaddress	4–25	ATM subaddress
Connection identifier	9	Identify connection resources
QoS parameter	6	Values for QoS request
Broadband sending complete	4–5	(Optional, for compatibility)
Transit network selection	4–8	Identify desired network
Endpoint reference	4–7	Identify endpoints of call

CALL PROCEEDING

This message indicates that the sender has received the information needed to process the call and will now do so. It is an acknowledgment of the SETUP.

CONNECT

This message is sent by the called party to show that the call has been accepted; it then propagates back through the network to the calling party.

CONNECT ACKNOWLEDGE

The network sends this message to the called party to acknowledge the connect message.

RELEASE

Either party can send the RELEASE message to terminate a call.

RELEASE ACKNOWLEDGE

When a call is torn down and the resources freed, this message is sent to inform the parties that the call is now dead.

Additional messages

There are a few more messages defined. They concern status enquiry (which we will not discuss) and multipoint virtual circuit setup, which will be discussed in Chapter 8.

4.9.3 Signaling Operations

For our discussion on signaling operations, consider the simple network shown in Figure 4-17. We have two computers (or end stations) and two switches. One computer will initiate a connection.

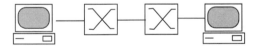

Figure 4-17. Sample signaling network.

Call setup

When a computer (the *calling party*) wants to make a connection to another computer (the *called party*), it sends a SETUP message to the switch it is connected to with the address of the destination machine, along with all of the other information needed in a SETUP message (Figure 4-18). Time flows down the diagram, with the calling party at the top left starting things off.

The switch passes the SETUP message along to the next switch, using its knowledge of the network topology and the hierarchical information in the

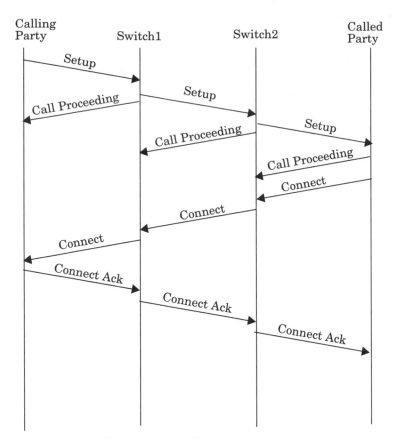

Figure 4-18. Call setup signaling.

addresses to pick the next switch, and may return a CALL PROCEEDING message indicating that it has all of the information it needs to make the call.

The SETUP message proceeds along to the called party, who optionally returns CALL PROCEEDING, examines the request to decide whether it will accept the call, and (assuming it does) eventually sends a CONNECT message. The CONNECT percolates back through the network. The calling party then sends a CONNECT ACKNOWLEDGE to the called party and setup is complete.

The VPI and VCI for the caller's end of the connection are selected by the first switch and sent to the calling party as part of the first CALL PROCEEDING message, if there is one, or as part of the CONNECT message, if not. If no circuits are available, a RELEASE COMPLETE with cause "No VCI Available" is sent instead.

As the SETUP wends its way through the maze of the network, the intermediate switches select circuits, and the called party is told what to use for its end of the connection. This is OK, since the switch choosing the VCI is the one the called party is connected to, and it "knows" all of the circuits the called machine is using.

Call clearing

When either party wishes to terminate the connection it sends a RELEASE message that proceeds similarly. When RELEASE COMPLETE is received, they know that the connection is gone (Figure 4-19).

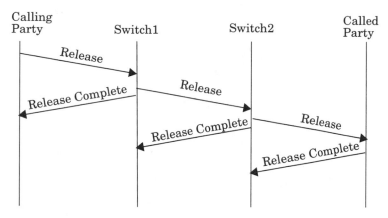

Figure 4-19. Call clearing signaling.

4.10 Network-to-Network Interface

Now knowing how the signaling works is all well and good, but how do the switches know how to send the calls along? There are several techniques, but the one most useful for the IP user is called the Private Network-to-Network Interface (PNNI). I am not going to describe the protocols in bit-level detail, but only enough so that you can understand what occurs in your network. If you need more detailed information the place to go is [ATM Forum 1994].

The PNNI is an interface between switches used to distribute information about the state and structure of the networks, to establish circuits, to ensure that reasonable bandwidth and QoS contracts can be established, and to provide for some network management functions.

The complex structure is managed by using an hierachical structure. Any given switch can be looked at as a plain switch or part of a larger virtual switching node, as shown in Figure 4-20. Here we see three views of a small network, with two hosts and interconnecting switches. In the top view we see what is the simplest version of the network: each host talks to a single node that it just thinks of as "The Network." Stepping down a level in the hierarchy it is revealed that there are in fact four nodes, all interconnected in some manner, and that the two hosts are really attached to two different nodes.

Finally, at the bottom of the figure, each of the four nodes of the previous level is seen to be further made up of multiple switches.

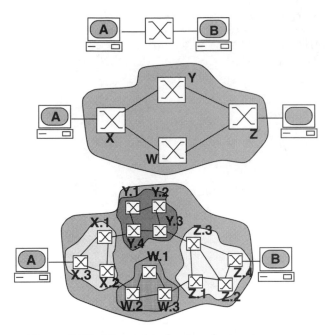

Figure 4-20. Hierarchical network structure.

So how does a host tell whether the "node" it is talking to is a real switch or a conglomerated "virtual switch"? In a sense it does not matter! All the host needs is to be able to send CALL_SETUP requests down its link to "The Network" and receive back CONNECT messages with the VCI to use. It does not care what the internal structure of the network is any more than someone does when they click on a WWW link and their IP packets get sent through 12 routers over six different networks to get to the server; as long as the data gets through it's happy.

So fine, the host does not need to know the structure of the network, but what about the switches? When host A sends a CALL_SETUP to X.3, asking it to please establish a connection to host B with this bandwidth, how does X.3 know the best path (or *any* path, for that matter) through the network to switch Z.4? How does X.3 even know it needs to get to switch Z.4 in the first place?

To solve this problem, the switches exchange information about the structure of the networks around them. To explain what happens we need to start at the bottom.

Peer groups

The hierarchical organization shown in Figure 4-20 prevents each switch from having complete knowledge of the structure of the network; needing to maintain such knowledge would render the routing unscalable. At a certain size, the tables of information would simply get too big to fit into the memory of the switch. It does not really matter how much memory there is in the switch either; eventually the network will grow to fill it. If we wish to build a scalable network that will allow unlimited growth, we need the hierarchy.

The lowest level switches are organized into *peer groups*. In the lowest portion of our diagram, the four switches next to host A would form a peer group. All of the members of a peer group exchange information with each other so that they all have the same information. Each peer group is assigned a *peer group ID* by the network administrator. Peer group IDs are a prefix of an ATM address. Usually this is the address of a switch (or all switches) in the peer group, but not necessarily.

Switches are configured so that they "know" whether the device on the other end of any given link is another switch or an end station. If it is a switch, then they periodically exchange *Hello Packets* to tell the other side what their peer group ID is (along with other information about the node). If they have the same peer group ID, then they can infer that they belong to the same peer group. By listening to these Hello messages, a given switch discovers when a neighboring switch becomes active. Because the messages are sent periodically, a switch can also infer that a neighboring switch has become inactive (or that the link has failed) by noting the failure of an expected Hello message to arrive.

Note that this implies that peer group IDs should be globally unique across the network. Since the regular ATM addresses are themselves globally unique, it makes sense to just assign addresses to the switches in a peer group such that their prefix is the peer group ID.

A well-known VCC is used for these Hello messages and for other PNNI message traffic.

Nodes collect information about the state of their neighbors and put them into packets called PNNI Topology State Elements (PTSEs). These PTSEs are flooded to all peer-group members; each node sends its own PTSE to all of its neighbors. When a node receives a PTSE from one neighbor it sends it to all of its other neighbors.

The PTSEs are not just blindly sent, however, for the algorithm I just described would result in PTSEs circulating in the peer group forever. What actually happens is that each node maintains a database of PTSEs that hold the current state of the network topology. Each PTSE has a version stamp. A node periodically sends PTSEs to its neighbors, who examine the version stamps. If it is the same version as the neighbor already has it does nothing except to acknowledge that the PTSE arrived intact. If the version is newer, however, the updated PTSE is installed in the neighbor's topology database and sent to its neighbors.

Thus we can see that if the PTSE migrates around a peer group and returns to a node that has already seen it, it will be discarded.

PTSEs age, and if they are not refreshed by the periodic updates, they are discarded.

Peer-group leaders

Moving up in the hierachical view of things, the peer group at the bottom of the hierarchy is seen to function as a "virtual switch" or logical group node (LGN) in the ATM Forum's terminology. Functions associated with being a LGN are performed by a distinguished node in the peer group called a Peer-Group Leader (PGL).

The peer-group leader is *elected* by the members of the peer group. The member of the peer group with the highest leadership priority becomes the leader. Base leadership priority is administratively assigned.

If two or more nodes have the same leadership priority, then the one with the highest node ID becomes the leader. In any case, the new leader's leadership priority is increased to ensure that it remains the leader and is not immediately deposed.

The PGL now represents the peer group in interactions with other peer groups, exchanging topology information with the PGLs of neighboring groups.

Logical group nodes

The peer group is now seen as a logical group node at a higher level of the hierarchy. The peer-group leader functions as a node in the higher level on behalf of the members of its peer-group. It summarizes the information gleaned from the PTSEs it collects into two items: a summary of the ATM addresses that can be reached in its peer group and a summary of the topology of the peer group. It sends these summaries to its peer LGNs, receives their summary reachability and topology information, and floods it to its peer-group members.

These LGNs aggregate into higher level peer groups and elect peer-group leaders in a similar fashion as the lowest level nodes.

Eventually we come to the top of the hierarchy and the concatenated networks look like a single logical (very large) node.

Border nodes

If two neighboring nodes exchange Hello messages and discover that they belong to different peer groups, then they become *border nodes*. Border nodes are the point of interconnection between a pair of peer groups. Note that they might not be the peer-group leaders.

The border nodes use the Hello protocol to exchange information about which peer groups they belong to and who their peer-group leaders are. This allows neighboring peer-group leaders to communicate, even if they do not have direct links to each other.

In our network diagram, nodes X.2 and W.2 are border nodes between the X and W LGNs.

Uplinks

In Figure 4-21, the previous diagram has been redrawn to show the levels of the hierarchy. Node Y is being ignored in this discussion for clarity.

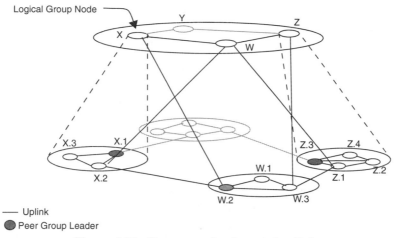

Figure 4-21. Peer-group leaders and uplinks.

The peer-group leader needs to know which border nodes provide connectivity to which other logical group nodes. In this diagram, node X.2 is the one that connects to LGN W. In order to tell the other nodes in LGN X this fact, node X.2 advertises an *uplink* to LGN W, which is sent to all its peer in group X. Similarly, X.2's neighbor across the border, W.2, advertises an uplink to LGN X to the rest of its group W peers [Guthrie 1967].

When X.1, the Peer Group Leader, wants to send its summarized topology and reachability information to its neighboring LGN W, it knows to send it to X.2 who will send it along the uplink to W. Similarly, W will send its information to W.2 to be sent up its uplink to X.

PNNI routing

Finally, let's see how a call from A to B gets routed. We start as node X.3 receives A's SETUP message. (We recall that X.3 is the switch that A is attached to.) Assume further that LGN Y is not suitable for this call, for whatever reason—perhaps it charges too much, perhaps its bandwidth is overcommitted.

Node X.3 needs to decide to which of its neighbors to route the call. It knows the destination ATM address, the topology of the local peer group, and it knows about the uplink to node W and the summarized topology information that came from node W. It can determine that the destination address lies somewhere in node Z, and that node Z can be reached through node W from this topology, so it sends the SETUP message on to node X.2, the border node, and base of the uplink. In PNNI, the first node in a peer group that a call reaches decides on the routing across the group.

Border node X.2 now knows from the information sent along with the call setup that is should now send the SETUP message to its border neighbor W.2.

W.2 is now in an analogous position to the one that X.3 was in. It knows the destination address is in LGN Z and that node W.3 is the border node to LGN Z, so it picks a route across the peer group, sends the SETUP to W.3, which sends it on to its neighbor Z.1.

Now we are in the peer group that contains the destination. Node Z.1 knows the topology of the peer group and that node Z.4 is the one that the destination is connected to. It chooses either Z.3 or Z.2 according to which is best suited to the parameters of the call. Whichever gets the SETUP sends it on to Z.4, knowing that Z.4 is the final-hop switch.

Z.4 sends the SETUP to host B, which (presumably) accepts the call and sends back a CONNECT message, which travels back through the network to A, at which point the call is established and data can flow. At last!

4.11 Permanent Virtual Circuits

All of this signaling looks very complicated, and it is. The complexity comes partly from its design by a committee that had to put in everything that everyone wanted, but mainly because it is trying to solve the hard problem of allocating resources fairly and never becoming confused.

Some people with simpler needs find using permanent virtual circuits (PVCs) attractive. If a network has only a handful of stations, it can be viable, but maintaining a mesh of PVCs in even a medium-size installation can get complicated quickly.

Consider that to fully interconnect, say, three hosts, two PVCs from each host connect to each of the other two hosts for a total of six. For four hosts, you need three PVCs from each of four hosts for a total of twelve. We added one host and *doubled* the number of PVCs needed.

Wait, it gets worse. In general, the number of PVCs needed for a mesh of N hosts is approximately N^2 [it's actually $N(N-1) = N^2 - N$, close enough for large N], so for 20 hosts you need 380 PVCs; for 100 hosts you need 9900!

When circuits have to be routed among multiple switches, keeping things straight can become a nightmare. There are several constraints on the circuits that all have to be satisfied at once:

- There should be N distinct VCs for each host to transmit on.
- The host must be configured to "know" which VCI goes to which destination host.
- If possible, a single mapping of VCIs to destinations is better than a different map for every host.
- Trunk VCIs must all be distinct. Remember that if you have two switches with M hosts on one and N on the other, you need $N*M$ VCs on the trunk between them!
- VCs should be densely allocated, so that limited VC space on some switch ports can be used efficiently.

This is not easy to keep straight! Some type of automated tool is needed that works well for medium-size (20–30) installations, but for an installation not much larger, the automated tool of signaled VCs is preferable.

4.12 Summary

ATM is a complex set of protocols. We looked at the broad background of B-ISDN and basic ATM concepts and examined the advantages of cell networking. We saw how switches work and what virtual circuits are. The set of Adaptation layers (AALs) was presented. After a discussion of ATM addresses we saw how circuits can be set up and torn down on demand. How these circuits are routed from switch to switch is the subject of PNNI routing, and we closed with a discussion of permanent virtual circuits.

Classical IP Over ATM

The IETF's scheme

Classical IP over ATM is a technique for achieving IP connectivity over ATM that was developed by the IP over ATM (ipatm) IETF working group. There are several RFCs that describe how it works:

- RFC 1483 Multiprotocol Encapsulation over ATM Adaptation Layer 5,
- RFC 1577 Classical IP and ARP over ATM,
- RFC 1626 Default IP MTU for use over ATM AAL5, and
- RFC 1755 ATM Signaling Support for IP over ATM.

An interesting document describing various models for carrying IP over ATM that have been considered is RFC 1932 [Cole 1996].

The purpose of Classical IP over ATM, or CIP as it is sometimes called, is to provide a way of using ATM technology as a direct replacement for LAN segments and local links. It can be thought of as "just another LAN technology" for this purpose. The idea of LAN Emulation (LANE), ATM technology pretending to be just like a LAN but faster, is not part of CIP. The IP Routing architecture used in the Internet remains intact.

How IP will be carried over ATM when a commercial worldwide ATM network is deployed is not addressed; the detailed nature of such a network was (and is) in too much of a state of flux to specify anything concrete.

Unlike LANE, CIP is not limited to the same packet sizes as the LAN it is replacing. This means, for instance, that the standard 8-kbyte NFS packets do not need to be fragmented (or reassembled) in the IP layer.

There are several parts to Classical IP over ATM. First, there is the method of encapsulating datagrams for transport. Next, there is a way to resolve IP addresses into ATM addresses so that connections can be established, and finally there are the signaling rules for setting up these connections.

5.1 Assumptions of CIP

The Classical IP scheme is predicated on several assumptions about the nature of the network being built.

First of all, the members of the Logical IP Subnet (LIS) must all have the same network number, subnet number, and address mask, or, in other words, they must all belong to the same subnet. Among other things, this means that packets can be efficiently routed to and from the LIS.

Each member of the LIS must be directly connected to the ATM network; they must have an ATM interface installed. Any computer not directly connected to the ATM network cannot be a part of this LIS and must not have the same subnet number.

Packets destined for addresses outside of the LIS must go through a router to get there; the router must be a member of the LIS. Naturally, packets from outside the LIS going to destinations inside must also go through the router.

If signaled virtual circuits are to be used, then the LIS members must be able to map IP addresses to ATM addresses in some way (see Section 5.5).

LIS members must be able to map VCs to IP addresses; that is, given one end of a VC, they need to figure out the IP address of the machine on the other end.

The LIS must be fully connected. Any member must be able to communicate directly, via ATM, with any other member.

And finally, a member of the LIS must know its own ATM address and that of the ATMARP server for the LIS.

5.2 MTU Size for IP Over ATM

Since IP fragmentation reduces performance [Kent 1987], it would be a good idea for the default MTU used for IP packets to be large enough that the packets of most common protocols would not be fragmented.

The preferred AAL, AAL5, will allow packets of up to 64 kbytes (less trailer overhead), so that is an upper limit on the size we can choose.

The Network File System protocol uses a default packet size of 8192 bytes, or 8 kbytes, and is in common use. Allowing for the various headers wrapped around this packet (RPC, UDP, IP, and LLC/SNAP), we can estimate that about 8300 bytes would be a good number.

It turns out that the IP MTU for Switched Multimegabit Data Services (SMDS) is defined as 9180 octets, which is close to our desired 8300. The IETF felt that there was no good reason for the ATM MTU to be different, since NFS packets will fit nicely into 9180, and that this will make connecting SMDS and ATM networks together easier—the routers involved will not have to fragment SMDS packets to send them into ATM, or vice versa.

This MTU is required to be used on networks using PVCs, but networks using signaled circuits are required to negotiate the MTU, so a larger MTU could be used if both hosts agree on it (or a smaller one, if the other host is a router forwarding onto a network with a smaller MTU, for instance).

5.3 Encapsulation of Datagrams in ATM PDUs

Two schemes for "connectionless datagram traffic" are defined by RFC1577.

The first, called *LLC Encapsulation*, allows multiple protocols to be carried over a single VCC. A header contains information that the receiver can use to determine which protocol will receive which packet.

The second scheme uses the ATM VCCs themselves to multiplex different protocols and is called *VC Based Multiplexing*. In this scheme, the receiver knows that when the connections are set up, a given VCC will carry IP packets, or that it will carry IPX, and so on. One VCC per protocol must be established.

In both schemes, datagrams are encapsulated in AAL5 PDUs. When using LLC encapsulation, a header is used to distinguish the protocol in use (Figure 5-1).

In practice, LLC-based encapsulation is usually used. The RFC specifies that it should be the default encapsulation and requires all implementations to support it.

The header affixed to the beginning of the packet is 8 bytes long. For most applications, this will be an LLC/SNAP header, which starts with 0xAA-AA-03. This is the LLC code for "SNAP header." Subnetwork access point (SNAP) headers are 5 bytes long, consisting of 3 bytes of OUI and 2 bytes of PID. If the Organizationally Unique Identifier (OUI) is 0x00-00-00, then the 2-byte PID is interpreted as an Ethertype. That is, the PID is coded with the same value that an Ethernet packet for this protocol would have in its Ethertype field.

Thus, when using LLC encapsulation, all packets will start with the sequence 0xAA-AA-03-00-00-00, followed by the Ethertype.

Typical values for this ethertype field are shown in Table 5-1.

Figure 5-1. Classical IP AAL5 datagram encapsulation.

Table 5-1. Typical Ethertypes.

Ethertype Value	Protocol Type
0x0800	IP
0x0200	PUP
0x0806	ARP
0x8035	RARP
0x0600	XNS

5.4 Classical IP with PVCs

Using permanent virtual circuits in an ATM network has its ups and downs. On the one hand, the client implementation is greatly simplified, because all that complicated signaling code can just be left out.

On the other hand, it can stress a network that has switches with limited numbers of PVCs allowed per port. In BAGNet [Johnston 1995], for instance, we found that the limiting factor on the size of the network was the number of PVCs allowed in Pacific Bell's interswitch trunks.

Administration overhead is greater with PVCs too, since virtual circuits must be assigned from every host, to every host, possibly through multiple

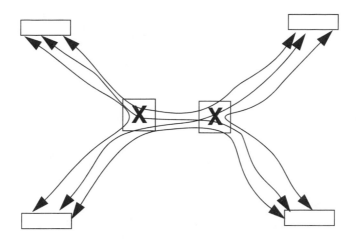

Figure 5-2. A complete PVC mesh—two switches, four hosts
(loopbacks omitted for clarity).

switches (Figure 5-2). This sounds easy to do, but it is harder than it looks, since
several constraints must be satisfied at once:

- Each host must have a unique VC on which to transmit to each of the other
  hosts.[1]
- Each host's allowable VCI range may be different due to implementation
  differences in ATM host adapters.
- Each VC that goes between two switches must have a VCI distinct from all
  other VCIs between those switches.
- Since most switches have a limited number of programmable VCIs, the
  VCIs between switches should preferably be dense; there should be no large
  gaps in the assigned values. Otherwise, one could just take, for instance, the
  endpoint IP addresses and switch IDs and concatenate them for a unique,
  though large, VCI.
- If PVCs are assigned with nontrivial quality of service specifications, the
  bandwidth assignments could exhaust the capacity of a given port for
  seldom-used links.

Even given these limitations, setting up a laboratory network of a few hosts
and one or two switches is not too hard, but maintaining even a medium-sized
network of four switches and 56 hosts[2] starts to become a nightmare without
automated tools to help. Unfortunately, such tools that work in a heterogeneous

---

[1] Even to itself—it is sometimes useful to be able to send traffic to yourself through the network, to ensure things are working correctly.

[2] The current size of the experimental ATM network at Xerox PARC, for which I wrote such a
tool.

installation are not available, so we must build them ourselves (or use signaling and avoid the whole problem, but we will deal with that in Section 5.5.

But enough of this digression. How does Classical IP work with PVCs?

Two configurations must be maintained: A host must know the table of which VCs are in use, and the mesh of PVCs through the switches must be established.

Once a host using this scheme appears, it needs to determine which PVCs are configured for it and which host is connected to the other end of each PVC.

In order for this to work, either the mapping of hosts to PVCs must be established by configuring the driver (done by the long-suffering system administrator) or the host must ask the host on the other end of each PVC to identify itself.

Luckily there is a protocol for doing this, called Inverse ARP (InARP) [RFC 1293]. Classical IP uses a variant called InATMARP. The packet format for InATMARP (and regular ATM ARP) is shown in Figure 5-3. The first three longwords of the packet are a header that contains the information that tells what this packet is for and describes the type and length of the various addresses being dealt with. Then the actual addresses follow.

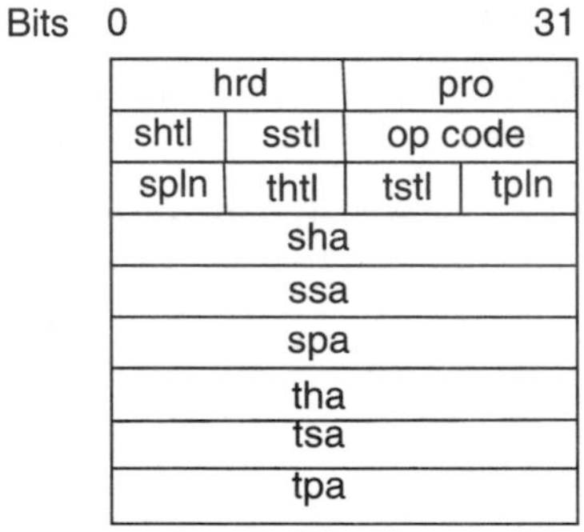

Figure 5-3. ATMARP packet format.

- **hrd.** is the code for the hardware type involved. Values assigned can be found in the latest "Assigned Numbers" RFC. 1 means 10 Mbit Ethernet, and 15 means Frame Relay, for instance. The value we want here for Classical IP is 19.
- **pro.** is the protocol type for the address we want. This is in fact identical to the Ethertype field used in LLC Encapsulation (see Table 5-1). For Classical IP this will be the ethertype value for IP, 0x0800.
- **shtl.** is the type and length of the source ATM number.
- **sstl.** is the type and length of the source ATM subaddress.
- **op code.** is the ARP operation being performed by this packet (see Section 5.5.1).
- **spln.** is the length of the source protocol address.

- **thtl.** is the type and length of the target ATM number.
- **tstl.** is the type and length of the target ATM subaddress.
- **tpln.** is the length of the target protocol address.

The rest of the fields are the addresses. **sha** is the source ATM number described by **shtl**; **tpa** is the target protocol address described by **tpln.**

The ATM addresses can be either ATM Forum NSAPA format or ITU E.164 format (Figure 5-4). Since the address type field is 8 bits, and ATM addresses are never more than 20 bytes (and 20 will fit into 5 of the bits), we can use the upper bits for coding. If the seventh bit is a 0, then it is an NSAPA, and if it is a 1, the address is E.164.

The length section tells how many bytes of address follow the header.

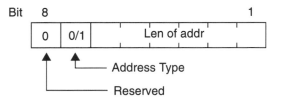

Figure 5-4. ATM address type and length coding.

5.5 Signaling the Circuits

5.5.1 The ARP Problem

Now, there's a problem here. When the driver for the ATM interface gets a packet to send, it only knows the destination IP address. Somehow this needs to be turned into a VCI for the packet to be sent on.

If you are using PVCs, there is a mapping between IP addresses and VCIs established when the PVC is set up that lets you send the packet, as described in the previous section.

If you are using SVCs, though, you first need to establish the circuit by sending a request to the switch—but the ATM switches do not understand IP addresses, only ATM addresses.

Given a destination IP address, how do you determine its ATM address so that you can ask the signaling code to set up a circuit?

The solution that IETF came up with was to have an "ARP" server on the LIS. Each machine must know its own IP and ATM addresses, and the ATM address of the ARP server must be configured.

When a machine boots (or at least, when it initializes its ATM network driver) it registers its addresses with the ARP server. When a machine needs to connect to another machine, it asked the ARP server, "What ATM address goes with this IP address?"

If the destination machine is registered, the ARP server's reply supplies an ATM address that can be used to create an SVC.

Note that if the destination machine is outside of the LIS, the routing code at the IP layer will notify the driver to send the packet to an LIS edge router; it will be the *router*'s IP address that gets looked up, and the router's ATM address that is returned.

Naturally, machines cache the ARP entries so that next time they need the ATM address of a host they need not go through this rigamarole again. The entries can age, get stale, and go away, though.

The entries in the ARP server that are created when a machine registers are valid for at least 20 minutes. After this time, the server will use InATMARP to check that the machine is still there; if it is, the 20 minute timer is reset. If not, the entry is discarded.

Client machines keep their entries for at the most 15 minutes, after which it is discarded. If there is an open VC to the destination, the entry can be revalidated with InATMARP too, but if there are no VCs, the entry must be removed.

5.5.2 Establishing the Circuit

So here we are in the ATM card's device driver, we have an IP packet to send, and we know the ATM address of the destination. Now what?

First we check to see if there already is a VC established to this destination that we can use. It is possible that there may be one already. Certainly, if we have recently talked to this host, there should still be a VCC hanging around.

However, it is possible that there may be a VCC to this destination that we cannot use. If an application has requested a connection with a certain quality of service so as to ensure that it can meet its performance goals, it may not want to share the connection with anyone else.

Assuming that a cached VCC is not available for general use, we invoke the ATM signaling code to establish a connection for us.

RFC 1755 specifies the information elements that are required for CIP connections. Table 5-2 shows the information elements that are required (MUST) and optional (MAY) in the SETUP message.

The AAL Parameters element tells which AAL should be used and the maximum size frame that should be carried. The AAL should be AAL5, and the frame size should be 65,535 for both forward and backward sizes. (The ITU allows each direction of a VC to have different parameters.)

The Broadband Low-Layer Information element selects the encapsulation to be used. LLC/SNAP is the default and is indicated with the assigned code for "lan_llc".

The Traffic Descriptor specifies the expected characteristics of the data traffic for the VC that is about to be created. It specifies forward and backward

Table 5-2. Classical IP signaling information elements.

Name	Status	Description
AAL Parameters	MUST	Which AAL, packet size
ATM Traffic Descriptor	MUST	Characteristics of traffic on this VCC
Broadband Bearer Capability	MUST	Traffic Class
Broadband Low-Layer Information	MUST	Encapsulation used
QoS Parameter	MUST	Unspecified QoS
Called Party Number	MUST	Destination ATM address
Calling Party Number	MUST	Source ATM address
Calling Party Subaddress	MAY	Endpoint or protocol specific
Called Party Subaddress	MAY	Endpoint or protocol specific
Transit Network Selection	MAY	How to get from here to there

peak cell rate as equal to the link rate and should specify "Best Effort Capability." This will allow IP packets to use as much of the network's bandwidth not committed to other circuits.

The Broadband Bearer Capability element specifies the traffic type, and the QoS element requests the desired parameters for Quality of Service.

The SETUP message must, of course, contain the address of the called party—one cannot set up a connection to someone without telling the network who it is! Optionally, a destination subaddress and the calling party's address may be included.

The last element is the optional Transit Network Selection, which can be used to choose among options for the network to carry this traffic, which is very much like choosing a long-distance carrier when a call is placed.

5.5.3 Circuit Maintenance and Aging

If an SVC is established for a given application, it will be torn down when that application finishes. However, if a general-purpose VC is established, it still needs to be torn down when it is no longer needed, but it's not so clear how to tell when that is.

RFC1755 suggests that as long as both endpoints of the VC are still operating, the VC should be held for *at least* 60 seconds after the "last" datagram, recommending 20 minutes. The holding time should be configurable in case administrators wish to minimize per-call charging from public networks or just want to time things out faster for policy reasons.

This way, VCs that are no longer needed will eventually disappear, freeing resources and ceasing to clutter up switches and host tables.

5.6 Classical IP Pros and Cons

The Classical IP scheme is well suited to IP-only networks and integrates well with the Internet model of how things should work. It requires significant modifications to network-level drivers to support ATMARP and InATMARP [Schuba 98], but luckily by now most workstation and personal computer ATM interface cards come with appropriate drivers already implemented.

Unlike LAN Emulation, Classical IP can operate without support for switched virtual circuits, which made a good choice for some early ATM field trials like BAGNET.

Also unlike LAN emulation, Classical IP can use large MTUs, eliminating IP packet fragmentation and boosting performance.

Classical IP's scalability is better than LAN Emulation's, particularly if multicast or broadcast support is needed (multicast and broadcast are not directly supported by RFC1577, but further IETF work expands on it as will be seen in Chapter 8.

However, non-IP protocols such as IPX or XNS are not supported at all. LAN Emulation operates at a lower level and will transport any packet that, say, an Ethernet will, and without changes to network drivers.

5.7 Summary

Classical IP is the IETF scheme for interconnecting IP-using hosts with ATM networks. It uses a Logical IP Subnet model to restrict the scope of the problem and defines an ATMARP mechanism for mapping IP addresses to ATM addresses. Large MTUs can be used. Support for permanent and switched virtual circuits is provided, and the parameters for the SETUP message are specified.

LAN Emulation

The ATM Forum's scheme

It is recognized that one of the keys to the widespread adoption of ATM is its ability to interoperate with existing networks, not like it was back in the early 1980s, when Ethernet was new and there were very few, if any, networks installed anywhere. To deploy a new network technology today, it must work with existing networks.

LAN Emulation (LANE) is the ATM Forum's attempt at a set of specifications to make this work for ATM and so-called "legacy" networks, Ethernet and Token Ring. The basic concept is that the ATM and LANE protocols look exactly like Ethernet or Token Ring to the existing computers and applications, while using the capabilities of the ATM network to provide higher performance.

Thus no changes to the protocols or applications on the existing computers need to be made, and LANE-compliant drivers provide identical interfaces (e.g., NDIS) to higher levels. In theory, just plug in a LANE hub, pop a new network card into the box, load the drivers from the card's diskettes and you are running ATM. Cool!

Of course, it is never quite that simple, but it is a worthy goal.

LANE does not attempt to translate Token Ring protocols into Ethernet or vice versa; an Emulated LAN must be one or the other, and if communication between them is desired, a router must get involved.

Phase One LANE is described below. Phase 2 was recently completed and addresses such things as server redundancy and fault tolerance. It will be summarized at the end of this chapter.

6.1 The LANE Pieces

There are several parts that make up an emulated LAN (ELAN) using LAN Emulation (Figure 6-1). Many of the ATM Forum documents refer to "entities"; these are software modules residing on hosts that process the LANE protocols.

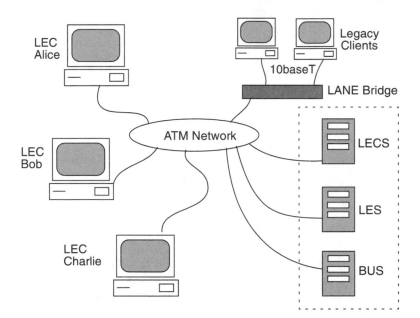

Figure 6-1. LAN emulation configuration.

6.1.1 LAN Emulation Client

The first entity is the LAN Emulation Client (LEC). This entity lives on LANE end systems. The LEC performs ATM address resolution and presents the standard LAN interface to the rest of the machine, masquerading as an Ethernet (or Token Ring). Every LEC must have a unique ATM address.

6.1.2 LAN Emulation Server

Next is the LAN Emulation Server (LES). There is one LES for each emulated LAN, and in fact to "belong to" an ELAN means to have a connection to that ELAN's server. Every LES must have a unique ATM address.

6.1.3 Broadcast and Unknown Server

The Broadcast and Unknown Server (BUS) handles broadcast and multicast traffic for a given LAN. While there can be more than one BUS in a given ELAN, Phase 1 LANE does not specify what this means, so one per ELAN is typical. Each client is assigned to a specific BUS (usually the only one!) that handles its broadcast and multicast traffic. Each BUS must have a unique ATM address, which the LES will associate with the broadcast MAC address ("all ones" or, e.g., FF:FF:FF:FF:FF:FF for Ethernet).

6.1.4 LAN Emulation Configuration Server

Finally, there's the LAN Emulation Configuration Server (LECS). It is extremely unfortunate that its acronym, LECS, is so close to the plural for LAN Emulation Client, LECs. Context should serve to keep them separate; when confusion might occur I will make sure to be careful to use unambiguous terms.

The configuration server's role is to assign newly initialized clients to the correct ELANs. It knows the proper LES for each one to connect to. There will be one LECS per "administrative domain" that will serve all the ELANs, whether Ethernet or Token Ring.

These server entities could reside in any machine attached to the ATM network, but will typically be found in switches or routers.

Since Phase 1 LANE only allows one BUS or LES per ELAN, it represents a single point of potential failure. Of course, since a BUS or LES usually resides in a switch, if the switch were to fail, the net would go down anyway. Phase 2 LANE specifies protocols to allow multiple redundant servers.

6.2 LANE Control Connections

These entities need to communicate with each other, of course. That is what as network is *for*, after all. A number of control connections are set up. The LEC is connected to the LECS, to the LES, and to the BUS (Figure 6-1).

Special connections are established so that these LANE Server entities can control the network. These are the control connections in an established ELAN:

- *Configuration-Direct VCC*: a bidirectional VCC set up by the LEC to the LECS so that it can figure out how to connect to its ELAN.
- *Control-Direct VCC*: a bidirectional VCC set up between the LEC and the LES so that the LEC can "register" with the LES.
- *Control-Distribute VCC*: a unidirectional multipoint VCC from the LES back to LECs.
- *Data-Direct VCC*: a bidirectional VCC connecting two LECs that wish to exchange data.

- *Multicast-Send VCC*: a unidirectional VCC from a LEC to the BUS, used by the LEC to send multicast and broadcast data.
- *Multicast-Forward VCC*: a unidirectional multipoint VCC from the BUS to all LECs, used to forward multicast and broadcast data.

In the case of ATM equipment that does not support multipoint VCCs, they can be simulated with a gaggle of point-to-point VCCs, though it is not as efficient.

6.3 LANE Operation

To see how LANE operates, watch a newly booted machine join an ELAN (already in progress).

6.3.1 Initialization

The ATM Forum defines five phases for the initialization of an LE Client:

1. LECS Connect Phase,
2. Configuration Phase,
3. Join Phase,
4. Initial Registration Phase, and
5. BUS connect Phase.

We will examine each on turn.

LECS connect phase

First, our LEC has to figure out its own ATM and MAC addresses. Usually the MAC address is in a ROM located on the network adapter card and is assigned by the manufacturer when the card is assembled. The ATM address is typically assigned by the system administrator.

Next, the LEC gets the LECS' ATM address by following a series of steps: First it must try to get the LECS address using ILMI (see Chapter 7). If that does not work, then it tries to use the "well-known" LECS address 47:00:79:00:00:00:00:00:00:00:00:00:00:A0:3E:00:00:001:00.[1] If success still eludes the LEC, it uses the standard preconfigured LECS PVC (VPI=0, VCI=17).

If there is still no luck, then the LECS Connect phase fails, a nasty message is displayed on the LEC screen and the system administrator gets a panicky phone call.

---

[1] But don't take *my* word for it. Check out the ATM Forum LANE documents. See? It *is* well known.

Armed with the address of the LECS, the initializing LE Client uses ATM UNI signaling to establish the Configuration-Direct VCC to the Configuration Server (LECS).

Configuration phase

The LEC tells the Configuration Server what its own ATM and MAC addresses are and then asks the LECS to tell it how to connect to its desired ELAN by sending a LE_CONFIGURE_REQUEST. It gets back a LE_CONFIGURE_REPLY message with all sorts of information: the ATM address of the correct LAN Emulation Server, the type of emulated LAN (Ethernet or Token Ring), the maximum packet size, and more. At this point the Configuration-direct VCC can be torn down.

Join phase

Now our plucky client establishes the control-direct VCC to the LES and receives its unique LEC Identifier. The LEC notifies the LES of its ATM and MAC addresses by sending a LE_JOIN_REQUEST message on the control-direct VCC. If all is well, the LES adds the LEC to the control-distribute VCC as a leaf. Even if all is not well, the LES sends back a LE_JOIN_REPLY to let the LEC know what happened. Unless more MAC addresses need to be registered with the LES, the LEC now tears down the control-direct VCC since it is no longer needed—the LES tells the LEC what to do from now on.

At this point, the LEC has joined its desired ELAN and has registered its MAC address with the LES.

Initial registration phase

This phase is optional. If the LEC wishes to register more MAC addresses with the LES, it can do so now by using the control-direct VCC it left open in the Join phase, by sending LE_REGISTER_REQUEST messages to the Server. The server returns LE_REGISTER_RESPONSE messages to let the Client know what happened.

BUS connect phase

Finally, the LEC asks the server what the ATM address of the BUS is by using the ARP protocol to get the address that corresponds to the all-ones MAC address (FF:FF:FF:FF:FF:FF). This MAC address is used for Ethernet broadcast, so it makes sense to use it for LANE broadcast too.

The LE client now establishes the multicast-send VCC to the BUS using this address and accepts a connection as it is added to the multicast-forward VCC as a leaf.

Figure 6-2 shows connections set up so far as 1–5. Now see how these clients can actually send data.

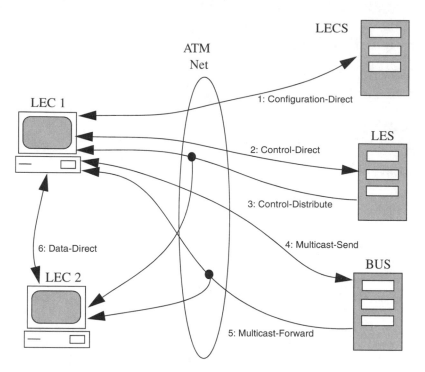

Figure 6-2. LANE connections for a client.

6.3.2 Data Flows

Imagine that LE Client Alice wants to send some data to another LE Client, Bob. Alice doesn't know Bob's ATM address, but does know his MAC address. Alice uses LAN Emulation ARP to ask the LES for Bob's ATM address. Alice assembles a packet with all sorts of things in it: her LEC ID, ATM address, MAC address, Bob's MAC address, and so on. If the server knows the ATM address that corresponds to Bob's MAC address, it sends a LE_ARP_RESPONSE back to Alice telling her that. If the server does not know it, Alice gets a NAK reply. (We are glossing over error conditions because they add a great deal of complexity to the discussion and obscure understanding of the basic operations. Suffice it to say that nearly everything that can go wrong has been thought of and how to deal with it has been specified.)

(Remember how the LEC asked the server for the BUS's ATM address? It did this by sending a LE_ARP message asking for the ATM address corresponding to the MAC address FF:FF:FF:FF:FF:FF, the broadcast address.)

Now if all went well, Alice has the ATM address of Bob and can use the signaling protocols to establish a data-direct VCC to Bob. Once this is accomplished, they can merrily send back and forth color 8x10 glossy packets with circles and arrows and a paragraph in the payload of each one.

When Alice and Bob are done, the data-direct VCC can be left around for a while in case they might want to exchange more data. In that case, the whole procedure is reduced to just looking up the VCC and shoveling the data out.

Now imagine that Charlie wants to send multicast data to Alice and Bob. That is easy—the multicast packets are sent over the multicast-direct VCC to the BUS, which in turn sends them to all the leaves of the multicast-forward tree.

This implies that Charlie will get back a copy of his own packet. Since some protocols cannot handle this, LANE requires that each host append their LECID to all multicast packets so that the Charlie's LANE driver can filter out his returning packets.

6.3.3 Shutdown

When a client decides to leave the ELAN, the procedure is fairly simple; it just clears all open VCCs and quits. The registered entries in servers are cleared, and the client must flush the ARP cache of all entries learned from the ELAN (since they will no longer work).

A server must not attempt to reach a client that has gone away; it is up to the client to try to reconnect. This makes sense, since if a client disappears because someone turns off their PC at the end of the day, we don't want the server to try all night to reconnect.

6.4 LANE Bridges

A LANE client can act as a bridge, forwarding frames to and from hosts and LAN segments that it is connected to. An example might be a box with an ATM port on one end and a dozen 10BaseT Ethernet ports on the other. All of the machines plugged into the Ethernet ports "think" they are talking to an Ethernet, but the bridge "knows" it is really connected to an ATM network. It performs LANE client services on behalf of the machines attached to it and sends notifications of topology changes to the LANE Server whenever its topology changes: machines come and go. The LES will propagate the topology information to other clients.

6.5 Pros and Cons

LANE is a Layer-2 bridging protocol; if you are of the Layer-3 router religions it is anathema and complicated. But it seems to work, at least for modest-sized networks. Scaling LANE to truly huge networks remains to be proven feasible.

It is really great if you have an overloaded backbone network connecting your workgroups. You can upgrade by putting in an ATM switch and replacing all of your 10baseT hubs with LANE bridges. The local workstations will still use 10baseT Ethernet to talk to the hubs, but now the backbone is 15 times faster.

Another nice feature is the support for Virtual LAN (VLANS). Using this technique one can create multiple networks that cannot talk with each other, which is great for maintaining security between groups. Furthermore, the VLANS can be geographically spread out and can traverse public networks, so that a server in Seoul could be accessed by a client in California as easily as if they were on the same LAN segment. With LANE, they are!

6.6 LANE Moves Ahead

The recent (July 1997) approval of the ATM Forum specifications for LANE v2 and Multiprotocol Over ATM (MPOA) are of interest and address some of the cons mentioned above.

6.6.1 LANE 2.0

Version 2.0 of LANE is described in [ATM Forum 1997a]. While operations are quite similar, it provides these enhancements to the basic LANE v1 facilities:

- Quality of Service (QoS). LANE v2 provides facilities for LECs to negotiate quality of service parameters. The Available Bit Rate (ABR) traffic class is supported. (See Section 9.1 for more on ABR.)
- Enhanced Multicast. LANE v2 provides mechanisms whereby multicast traffic can be separated from unicast traffic; not all hosts in the ELAN must receive all the multicast traffic (and perhaps discard it), only "interested" hosts will. (See Chapter 8 for more on multicast.)
- Multiprotocol Over ATM (MPOA). LANE v2 adds support for MPOA, described in the next section.

6.6.2 MPOA

Multiprotocol Over ATM (MPOA) allows LANE devices to operate across subnets with ATM virtual connections, alleviating the drawbacks of LANE's bridging-only architecture and allowing operation in Next Hop Routing Protocol (NHRP) clouds. (See Section 7.4.1 for a description of NHRP.) MPOA is fully described in [ATMForum 1997b].

MPOA requires LANE 2.0, UNI signaling, and NHRP. Two kinds of MPOA machines are needed: MPOA Clients (MPCs) and MPOA Servers (MPSs).

MPCs include a LANE client as a component. An MPC acts in two roles: ingress and egress. In the ingress role it observes packet flows and establishes shortcuts for flows that pass through an MPS and uses MPOA queries to the MPOA server to establish a shortcut virtual circuit to the flow's destination, if possible. This shortcut virtual circuit could cut across several subnets, in effect bypassing the intermediate routers altogether.

In the egress role, the MPC forwards frames from other hosts, adding or changing appropriate encapsulations for frames received over shortcuts.

An MPS includes an NHRP Next Hop Server (NHS) as a component. It receives MPOA queries and answers them by using NHRP to communicate with other MPSs and NHRP-supporting routers. It provides shortcut information to ingress MPCs and encapsulation information to egress MPCs. (Of course, the same MPC might act as both an ingress and egress device.)

6.7 Summary

LAN Emulation is the ATM Forum's solution for hooking up computers to ATM networks. It uses switched circuits to interconnect machines and transparently bridges their packets across the ATM network. A configuration server keeps track of everything, and a broadcast server handles broadcast packets by retransmitting them to all clients.

Managing the Mess

So far, you have probably realized that ATM, whether using the IETF flavor or the ATM Forum flavor, is a complicated beast.

So that order might be brought out of chaos, some sort of management of the pieces is necessary.

7.1 What Is Network Management?

From time to time, the administrator of a network needs to perform certain tasks in order to keep things working. These include:

- *Configuration Management*: The administrator needs to be able to enable and disable ports on a switch when machines are added to or removed from the network.
- *Fault Management*: Automatic detection of faults, like loss of signal or hardware failures, is extremely valuable. Even being able to ask the equipment what is going on helps a great deal.
- *Statistics Collection and Performance Monitoring*: Prudent administrators keep track of what is happening on their networks to be able to spot bottlenecks and to plan for future capacity upgrades.

- *Connection Management*: In a world where ATM connections may be charged by the minute (or kilocell), it would be silly not to keep track of what connections are made to where and for how long. Even in an unmetered local network it is important to be able to diagnose connection problems.

7.2 Simple Network Management Protocol (SNMP)

The Simple Network Management Protocol (SNMP) was developed as a foundation for building network management tools. The protocol itself is indeed quite simple, and is defined in RFC 1157. An excellent introduction to SNMP is [Rose 1996].

Actual use of the protocol, however, can get as complex as the information being managed.

7.2.1 SNMP Data Structures

SNMP data is stored in and accessed through Management Information Bases (MIBs). These are hierarchically organized data structures with publicly known structures. As a concrete example, a simple workstation with an Ethernet interface might have an MIB containing the Ethernet address, IP address, input and output packet counts, whether the interface was up or down, and so on.[1]

MIBs are described using a subset of the Abstract Syntax Notation One (ASN.1) language. This is an ISO language (ITU X.208/ISO 8824) that is useful for representing data structures in a portable way.

As an example, here is the beginning of the Internet MIB defined in RFC 1156 (and required of all Internet hosts that implement SNMP).

The Internet MIB (extract)

```
RFC1156-MIB
DEFINITIONS ::= BEGIN
IMPORTS
    mgmt, OBJECT-TYPE, NetworkAddress, IpAddress,
    Counter, Gauge, TimeTicks
      FROM RFC1155-SMI;

mib          OBJECT IDENTIFIER ::= { mgmt 1 }
```

---

[1] Of course it is of limited utility to a remote administrator to ask whether the interface is "up" when it is in fact "down," but the lack of response itself is significant, and it *is* useful locally, or for multi-homed machines.

```
system      OBJECT IDENTIFIER ::= { mib 1 }
interfaces  OBJECT IDENTIFIER ::= { mib 2 }
at          OBJECT IDENTIFIER ::= { mib 3 }
ip          OBJECT IDENTIFIER ::= { mib 4 }
icmp        OBJECT IDENTIFIER ::= { mib 5 }
tcp         OBJECT IDENTIFIER ::= { mib 6 }
udp         OBJECT IDENTIFIER ::= { mib 7 }
egp         OBJECT IDENTIFIER ::= { mib 8 }
END
```

Here we see several things that illustrate ASN.1:

- The MIB has a name (RFC1156-MIB).
- Its definitions are enclosed in BEGIN-END keywords.
- It imports definitions from other MIBS (such as mgmt).
- It defines OBJECT IDENTIFIERS that become part of this MIB.

This last concept, the Object Identifier (OID), is an important one for understanding SNMP. Each SNMP object has a hierarchical identifier assigned to it. The ISO administers all OIDs that begin with 1, the ITU ones that start with 0. A subtree under 1 is designated for other organizations (1.3), and 1 is assigned to the U.S. Department of Defense (1.3.6), which has assigned a node to the Internet Architecture Board (1.3.6.1) (Figure 7-1).

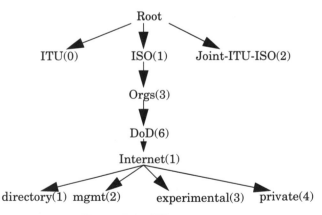

Figure 7-1. OID structure.

Thus all OIDs assigned by the IETF under the aegis of the IAB start with 1.3.6.1 (and any OID that starts 1.3.6.1 must have been assigned by the IETF). It is very convenient that sections of OID space can be assigned to organizations that can then use them as they see fit; not having to negotiate an international treaty to change a field from 8 bits to 16 bits saves a great deal of time.

The management node of the internet hierarchy is imported from
RFC1155-SMI and has OID 1.3.6.1.2. Therefore, when in our example we see

```
mib            OBJECT IDENTIFIER ::= { mgmt 1 }
```

that declares our mib to be "mgmt.1" or 1.3.6.1.2.1.

Later, when we see

```
system         OBJECT IDENTIFIER ::= { mib 1 }
```

we have defined a new object dependent on our mib object, which will have OID
1.3.6.1.2.1.1. And so on…

So far we are just carving up OID space into chunks. Eventually we have to
get to some real data.

SNMP uses only a few data types from ASN.1, as shown in Table 7-1, and
uses the SEQUENCE and CHOICE operators to define more complex types. A
Sequence is an ordered list of items, similar to what C calls a struct or Pascal
calls a record, and a CHOICE is like a C union.

Table 7-1. ASN.1 primitive types used by SNMP.

Type	Code	Use
INTEGER	2	Numbers
OCTET STRING	4	Strings
OBJECT IDENTIFIER	6	MIB variable ID
NULL	5	Arbitrary data

The data are represented using a "Type, Length, Value" coding as specified
by the ASN.1 Basic Encoding Rules (BER). The first byte is a code telling the
type of the data item, then the length is coded. If the high bit of the first length
byte is a 0, then the length is between 0 and 127 (which fits into the remaining 7
bits of the byte). If the high bit of the first length byte is a 1, however, the rest of
the byte tells how many following bytes make up the length. For example, 128
would be coded as 0x81-80 (Figure 7-2). It should be noted that quite long data
items can be coded this way. The "length of the length" field can hold 7 bits, so
the length field proper can be up to 127 bytes long. For an INTEGER type, that
would be truly enormous.[2]

A few standard types are defined by RFC 1155, such as NetworkAddress,
IpAddress, Counter, Gauge, TimeTicks, and Opaque.

---

[2] 127 * 8 bit/byte = 1016 bytes of length, which can encode a length of $2^{8128} - 1$, but who's
counting?

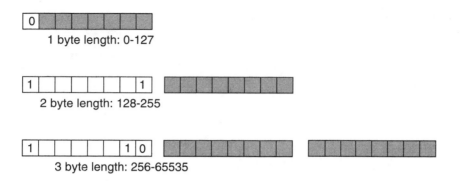

Figure 7-2. ASN.1 length coding.

So, as a more concrete example of real objects, look at the *System Group* part of the Internet MIB:

The System Group

```
-- the System Group
-- Implementation of the System group is mandatory for all
-- systems.  If an agent is not configured to have a value
-- for any of these variables, a string of length 0 is
-- returned.


sysDescr OBJECT-TYPE
    SYNTAX  DisplayString (SIZE (0..255))
    ACCESS  read-only
    STATUS  mandatory
    DESCRIPTION
      "A textual description of the entity.  This value
       should include the full name and version
       identification of the system's hardware type,
       software operating-system, and networking
       software.  It is mandatory that this only contain
       printable ASCII characters."
            ::= { system 1 }


sysObjectID OBJECT-TYPE
    SYNTAX  OBJECT IDENTIFIER
    ACCESS  read-only
```

```
     STATUS   mandatory
     DESCRIPTION
        "The vendor's authoritative identification of the
        network management subsystem contained in the
        entity.  This value is allocated within the SMI
        enterprises subtree (1.3.6.1.4.1) and provides an
        easy and unambiguous means for determining `what
        kind of box' is being managed.  For example, if
        vendor `Flintstones, Inc.' was assigned the
        subtree 1.3.6.1.4.1.4242, it could assign the
        identifier 1.3.6.1.4.1.4242.1.1 to its `Fred
        Router'."
           ::= { system 2 }


sysUpTime OBJECT-TYPE
     SYNTAX   TimeTicks
     ACCESS   read-only
     STATUS   mandatory
     DESCRIPTION
        "The time (in hundredths of a second) since the
        network management portion of the system was last
        reinitialized."
           ::= { system 3 }


sysContact OBJECT-TYPE
     SYNTAX   DisplayString (SIZE (0..255))
     ACCESS   read-write
     STATUS   mandatory
     DESCRIPTION
        "The textual identification of the contact person
        for this managed node, together with information
        on how to contact this person."
           ::= { system 4 }


 (...)
```

Notice several features of this notation:

- Each object has a name specified by an OBJECT-TYPE.
- Each object has a SYNTAX, the data type corresponding to this object.
- Each object has an ACCESS field, describing whether it can be read or written (or both).
- Each object has a STATUS, whether it *must* be implemented or is optional.
- Each object has a DESCRIPTION, explaining what it is.
- Each object has an *Object Identifier* associated with it.

For example, the sysUpTime is an object of type TimeTicks, whose OID is "system.1". "System" is "mgmt.1", and "mgmt" is 1.3.6.1.2, so the sysUpTime OID is 1.3.6.1.2.1.1.

Note: The MIB most widely used for TCP/IP equipment is called "MIB-2" and is described in RFC 1213.

7.2.2 SNMP Protocol

Well, now we can name things. We can build data structures, and every manufacturer can be (and is if they ask for one) assigned a node in the "enterprises" tree, so they can build custom MIBS to suit their gear. Now what?

Now we see how machines can talk to each other and exchange information. Imagine that a workstation named scylla wants to query a router named charybdis and find out which interfaces are up. I am not going to go into bit-level detail about the format of the messages, since that is not really relevant here, and we want to get on to how this relates to ATM.

The basic interaction of SNMP occurs when scylla builds a packet to send to charybdis to ask it a question. Since this is a request to get some information, the packet is called a GetRequest.

The GetRequest packet contains an integer RequestID and a list of variable bindings. The variable bindings consist of pairs of Object Identifiers and the syntax for their value. For instance, if scylla wants to ask charybdis how long it has been up, it would sent the GetRequest with the OID for the sysUpTime and the syntax for the TimeTicks (which happens to be an unsigned 32-bit integer.)

Charybdis receives this GetRequest packet and transforms it into a GetResponse packet with the same RequestID, which it sends back, with the variable bindings replaced with the current values of those objects.

Notice that by including the RequestID in the response, multiple queries can be outstanding and scylla will be able to sort out which response goes with which request as they arrive.

Naturally, there are specifications for dealing with all kinds of errors, but I'll gloss over these here. Interested parties can consult the references for the details.

Another type of request is the GetNextRequest, used for examining tables of information (a router's routing table, for instance).

The SetRequest message is similar to the GetRequest, but instead of asking the destination what value it has, we give it a new value.

The final kind of SNMP message is the Trap, which is spontaneously generated by SNMP-managed equipment and sent to a management host. If charybdis were to suddenly crash and reboot, it might send a coldStart trap to scylla, the management host configured in its ROM, when it came up again so that scylla would know that something happened. Other standard traps include warmStart, linkDown ("Help! Someone just unplugged a cable!"), linkUp ("It's OK, they plugged it back in again!"), authenticationFailure ("Someone's trying to crack me!") and egpNeighborLoss ("My EGP routing neighbor scylla just went away!").

Of course, some sort of authentication for SetRequests must be done. If we let a router or switch or other piece of gear accept SetRequest messages from any source, anyone in the greater Internet could wreak havoc with our net. For whatever reason, too, an organization may wish to restrict GetRequests as well, on the theory that it is no one else's business how their internal network is configured.

SNMP entities are organized into communities, which are identified with a string called the Community Name. When an SNMP agent needs to send a message, it constructs the message and has its local authenticator prepare an authentication object, which it adds to the message to be sent. The recipient takes the message, extracts the authentication object and community name, and decides whether the message is authentic and should be obeyed.

The authentication can be implemented in many ways; one of the most common is to have no authentication at all! A slightly tighter scheme is to only accept SetRequests from hosts on the same subnet, and a quite effective scheme might involve some sort of cryptographic signature proving that the sender is indeed authorized to meddle with the innards of the recipient. As the Internet grows, it gets its share of good guys and bad guys like any other community, and users have to start locking their metaphorical doors by making at least their gateway routers and firewalls secure against attacks.

7.3 Interim Local Management Interface

The ATM Forum defined the Interim Local Management Interface (ILMI) [ATM Forum 1996] as a stopgap measure until the official standard is produced by the ITU-T. ILMI uses the SNMP message format to transfer its information, which is why we had to read through that long discussion on SNMP.

ILMI does not, however, use UDP for message transport as "plain" SNMP does, nor does IP come into the equation at all. ILMI messages are packaged up with AAL5 and sent over a specified virtual connection, which defaults to VPI=0,

VCI=16. Like the speaking tubes on the bridge of the battleship in those old war movies, this one goes to the engine room, this one goes to fire control, and so on. This VC (0/16) goes to the ILMI entity on the other end of the connection, that one (0/5) is for signaling, and so on.

ILMI is intended to be an open protocol, so the public standard SNMP was chosen for it rather than developing a new private protocol.

ILMI defines four MIB modules for ATM devices. They are:

1.   Textual Conventions MIB,
2.   Link Management MIB,
3.   Address Registration MIB, and
4.   Service Registry MIB.

7.3.1 Textual Conventions

The Textual Conventions MIB is a sort of catch-all place where definitions of objects used by the other three are kept. Items such as AtmAddress, NetPrefix, and traffic types are defined here.

- **AtmServiceCategory:** This is an INTEGER that indicates a class of ATM service. CBR, ABR, UBR, real-time and non-real-time VBR, and "other" are the possibilities.
- **AtmAddress:** ATM addresses are represented as OCTET STRINGS of either 8 bytes for native E.164 encoded addresses or 20 bytes for NSAP encoding.
- **NetPrefix:** An ATM network prefix is similarly coded as an OCTET STRING of either 8 bytes for native E.164 or 13 bytes for NSAP encoding.
- **OIDs and MIB Group:** ILMI defines several groups of OIDs as the "trunk" of the object tree that represents ATM management. We can see in Figure 7-3 how an OID subtree can be "grafted" onto the standard RFC-1213 tree.

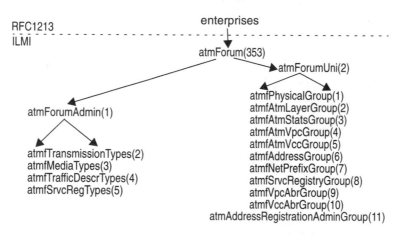

Figure 7-3. ATM Forum MIB groups.

These OIDs also define the structure and organization of the rest of the MIB.

- **QoS parameter coding:** This defines how we represent Quality of Service in messages. There are four types of QoS defined, as shown in Table 7-2.

Table 7-2. Traffic class parameter vectors.

Traffic Type	OID Symbol	Param 2	Param 2	Param 3	Param 4	Param 5
SCR/No CLP	atmfNoClpScr	Peak Cell Rate	Sustainable Cell Rate	Max Burst	CDVT	-
CLP/no tagging	atmfClpNoTaggingScr	Peak Cell Rate	Sustainable Cell Rate	Max Burst	CDVT	-
CLP w/tagging	atmfClpTaggingScr	Peak Cell Rate	Sustainable cell rate	Max Burst	CDVT	-
ABR	atmfClpNoTaggingMcr	PeakCell Rate	CDVT	min cell rate	-	-

When a station makes a call with a given set of QoS parameters, it is in effect promising the network certain things:

- "Peak Cell Rate" means "I will never send more than this many cells per second.
- "Sustainable Cell Rate" means "I expect to send about this many cells per second most of the time."
- "Maximum Burst Size" means "I will never send more than this many cells in one burst."
- "CDVT" is cell-delay variation; the difference in cell arrival times will never vary more than this many microseconds.

7.3.2 Link Management

The Link Management MIB provides general ATM interface-management capabilities. There are attributes and statistics for physical interfaces, ATM layer interfaces, and virtual paths and channels.

7.3.3 Address Registration

The Address Registration MIB allows registration of UNI addresses.

When a new host appears, first the network side (the switch) registers network prefixes with the user side (the host) by sending a SetRequest ILMI message. Then the host assembles complete ATM addresses out of the network prefix and the End Station Identifier (ESI) and perhaps a selector (SEL) field. Once a complete address is built, the host registers it with the network (i.e., its nearest switch).

While a host is connected to the network, it may create or delete additional ATM addresses; some implementations may wish to assign distinct addresses to different services or components. An ATM-based video encoder that can encode multiple video streams could register a separate address for each stream if it wished.

Finally, if the network notices that a host has disappeared (by observing that the light on the other end of the fiber has gone out, for instance, which generates a boatload of SONET errors) all of the addresses associated with that host are "deregistered." If the machine's owner simply tripped over the fiber and plugs it back in, the entire registration process has to start over. On the other hand, if the machine is moved to another part of the network and then plugged back in, having the old addresses automatically purged is essential.

7.3.4 Service Registry

The Service Registry MIB is used for locating ATM network services (such as a LAN Emulation Configuration Server). When a LECS or other server initializes, it can register itself with the network, and subsequent clients wishing to discover the address of the service can retrieve it using the ILMI protocols.

7.3.5 ILMI Procedures

Here are some of the things that can be done using ILMI.

Connectivity

Stations implementing ILMI are required to make sure that their peer ILMI entity still exists by issuing a getRequest message every 5 sec for atmfPort-MyIfIdentifier, atmfMySystemIdentifier, and sysUpTime. If no response arrives for four consecutive polls, the ILMI link is declared dead.

Automatic configuration

When an entity is configuring itself, it can decide whether to use the Private or Public UNI and whether to automatically behave as a "user"- or a "network"-type entity, based on information about its own type and that of its peer. The decision criteria are summarized in Table 7-3.

Note that connecting two user devices is undefined. This makes sense, since the signaling protocols assume that there is a "network" between any two end stations. If the local interface is a "user," then the station should use the user

Table 7-3.

Local Type	Peer Type	Peer Unit	resulting Interface Type
user	user	-	undefined
user	node	public	public UNI, user side
user	node	private	private UNI, user side
user	other	public	public UNI, user side
user	other	private	private UNI, user side
node	user	public	undefined
node	user	private	private UNI, network side
node	node	public	public UNI, user side
node	node	private	IISP or PNNI
node	other	public	public UNI, user-side
node	other	private	private UNI, network side

side of either public or private UNI, depending on the public- or private-ness of the peer.

If the station configuring itself is a node [(ATM Forum-ese for "switch (or other ATM Device not an end station)"] then if it is talking to another node that is private, it uses either IISP or PNNI, depending on which one the remote node implements. If it's talking to a public user, the result is undefined. If it is talking to a private station and not a node, then it uses private UNI, network side. Finally, if its peer is a public node, it uses user-side public UNI, and if it is a public something else, it uses public UNI network side.

Whew.

Modifying local parameters

When local parameters are modified, certain steps have to be taken. If the parameters were merely changes to the virtual circuit groups, such as changing the maximum VCI for signaled connections, all that is necessary is that the peer entity be notified through an ILMI/SNMP Trap.

However, if anything else is changed it is pretty much a disaster as far as the network is concerned. The ILMI document requires that the entity basically close all connections, reboot itself, and start again from scratch.

7.4 Routing in ATM Networks

Several approaches to routing in ATM networks have been proposed. The ATM Forum's Private Network-Node Interface (PNNI) has been discussed in Section 4.10. We will discuss a work in progress by the IETF here.

7.4.1 NHRP

The NBMA Next-Hop Routing Protocol (NHRP) is intended to be used in what the IETF calls Non-broadcast Multiple Access (NBMA) networks [Luciani97]. A nonbroadcast network is one that does not support broadcasting of packets. X.25 networks, for instance, have no ways of doing this, and in a large extended Ethernet it might be impractical.

Despite IETF and LANE broadcast services, ATM itself does not have a way of broadcasting packets to all attached hosts either, which makes NHRP quite relevant for our purposes. In the NBMA network model, the greater network can be divided into "logical NBMA subnetworks," which are much the same as the Classical IP Logical IP Subnet (LIS).

The main thing that NHRP does is to resolve IP (or other Layer-3) addresses into ATM (or other NBMA) addresses. We'll stick with IP and ATM, but remember that NHRP can be used with other address families as well.

So far it sounds much like ATMARP from Classical IP over ATM as discussed in Chapter 5. That is true, and NHRP can be used as a replacement for it, but it does more too. Using NHRP, we can discover the correct machine to connect to in order to get out of our NBMA.

Consider the networks shown in Figure 7-4. Imagine that host $a1$ on LIS A wants to send a packet to server $c4$ on LIS C. Further, the routers have the preconfigured connections as shown by the dotted lines. Host $a1$'s default router is set up as $Ra2$, perhaps because that is the gateway to the rest of the Internet. Router $Ra2$ has a link to router $Ra1$, and $Ra1$ has a link to router Rab, and so on. These could be the default routes set up by the network administrator to provide minimal connectivity.

Now, since we know from the characteristics of the LIS that any host on the LIS can connect to any other host on the LIS, and since *we* have perfect knowledge of the topology, it is easy to see that host $a1$ should establish a direct connection to router Rab to minimize the hops across its own LIS. The hard part is for host $a1$ to discover router Rab's ATM address so that it can make this connection!

Here is the way that host $a1$ can use NHRP to figure this out. First, for whatever reason, host $a1$ decides that it needs to send a packet to host $c4$. Host $a1$'s IP layer driver looks in its routing table and sees that its default route is to router $Ra2$, so it sends the packet down to the ATM driver with instructions to send it to $Ra2$. The ATM driver then looks in its next-hop cache for destination $c4$

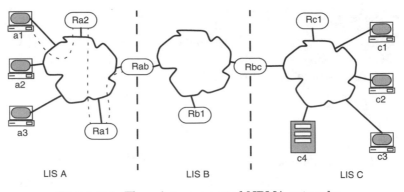

Figure 7-4. Three interconnected NBMA networks.

and finds nothing, so it builds a Next-Hop Resolution Request packet and sends it along to router *Ra2*, the current best guess.

At this point we need to decide what to do with the packet that is waiting to be sent to host *c4*. There are three choices:

1. drop the packet and forget about it,
2. hold the packet and wait until the NHRP response comes back, or
3. forward the packet to the current-best router.

Any of these is acceptable to some degree or another. Dropping the packet means that the upper layer protocol will have to notice that the packet is lost and retransmit it after some time-out; having your network always drop the first packet to a new host could be annoying.

Holding the packet until a response comes back could be considered better, but it means being prepared to buffer packets in the driver for a long time; and before the response comes they may still time out and be retransmitted anyway; now we have to buffer *two* packets.

The current draft of NHRP suggests that sending the packet on along the routed path (to *Ra2* in our example) is the best choice; at least the packets can start flowing along *some* path while the network figures out the "best" path.

Next, the NHRP request arrives at router *Ra2*. In this example we are assuming that all of the routers implement Next Hop Servers (NHS), entities that perform the NHRP. The NHS are tightly coupled to routers, but not all routers need to implement NHRP. It is necessary that the hosts using the service [Next Hop Clients (NHCs)] "know" at least one NHS they can send requests to; in this example, since all routers are NHSs, a host can just send the request to its default router.

The NHS on router *Ra2* now looks at the request and sees that host a1 is asking for the next hop to destination *c4*. *Ra2* does not know this, but its routing tables say to send traffic for *c4* to *Ra1*, so off goes the request. *Ra1*, similarly, forwards the request to *Rab*, the border router between LIS A and LIS B.

Now the NHS on *Rab* examines the request and decides from its routing tables that it is in fact the right place to send traffic for host *c4*, so it sends a Next Hop Resolution Reply back to host *a1*, which can now establish an SVC to router Rab for the remainder of its traffic to host *c4*.

However, at this point, router *Rab* looks in its Next-Hop cache and discovers that it does not know the *next* hop toward host *c4*; that is, the best hop across LIS B. It starts forwarding packets along the default route to host *c4* and issues its own Nest Hop Resolution Request.[3] Eventually a response comes back from router *Rbc*, and router *Rab* can make a direct connection across LIS B.

Finally router *Rbc* uses NHRP to determine the address of the "next hop" to host *c4*, which, since *c4* is on the same LIS as router *Rbc*, is just *c4*'s own address. Router *Rbc* can make a direct connection to host *c4* for the last hop, and we have a minimal path of three hops across the three interconnected LISs.

This is all well and good, but how do the NHS learn the information they need to make these decisions? From several sources:

- Hosts register with their nearest NHS when they bring up the ATM interface, much as they register with an ATMARP server in Classical IP over ATM. Indeed, an NHS can replace a CIP ATMARP server.
- NHSs can glean information about the network topology by examining the data in Next Hop Requests and Next Hop Reply packets that they forward.
- Data can be loaded into preconfigured tables by the network administrator.

7.5 What About Firewalls?

A *firewall* is a device, whether hardware or software, that allows network administrators to enforce an access policy regarding their networks. A company may decide to allow its employees to create FTP connections from their computers to the outside world, but to forbid FTPs from the outside world to any internal hosts. Mail might be permitted in both ways, but Telnet and rlogin forbidden, and so on.

These firewalls are becoming more and more common as the Internet grows, and companies connect up and discover that not only are there bad people out there that love to cause trouble, but their competitors might gain access to confidential information held on internal machines. Firewalls (or at least some form of access control) are rapidly becoming part of standard "due diligence" in

---

[3] Since this turns out to be a router-to-router link special care is needed to avoid stable routing loops; this is beyond our scope but those interested can read the relevant Internet Draft: draft-ietf-ion-r2r-nhrp-00.txt is the current version.

protecting company assets, much like locks on the doors and visitor sign-in requirements.

Getting back to networking, though, there is a problem with having a fire-wall between your ATM network and the outside world's public ATM network. On the one hand, if you allow signaled ATM connections through your firewall, you lose, because you now have arbitrary connections from who-knows-where penetrating your security layer. If you *do not* allow them, you lose because the firewall router is now a bottleneck and may not be able to keep up with the ATM stream. Standard routers will have to reassemble all of the packets from the cell stream, route them, and then shred them into packets again.

This problem has been addressed by a few researchers, but perhaps most cogently in [Lyles 96]. The authors identify five pieces that must be present for an effective firewall and discuss how to achieve them without falling into either of the pits described above.

The five elements are:

1. *Endpoint Authentication*: A given entity wishing to make a connection must be able to authenticate itself, that is, to prove that it is indeed who it claims to be. There are a large number of ways to provide authentication, such as Kerberos [Miller 1987], public key authentication [Merkle 1978] and so on, widely described in the literature. See, for example, [Kaufman 95].

2. *Domain Based Call Admission Control*: A host needs to be able to decide whether to accept or reject any given call, based on the identities of the endpoints and the established security policies. "Domain-based" means that hierarchical solutions to scaling problems can be applied. For example, I might want to allow members of my lab to read and write project files and members of my company to read but not write to them, but allow outsiders no access at all.

3. *Connection Authentication*: Once the endpoints of a connection have been authenticated, and a call has been allowed and connected, one still needs to make sure that the data flowing along that connection actually came from the originator of the call and that it goes to the proper receiver.

4. *Audit*: All of the pieces of the system should be able to log information about their activities. This is useful for purposes such as billing, intrusion detection, etc.

5. *Centralized Policy with Distributed Service and Enforcement*: Finally, for scalability, it is important that the actual performance of these features be distributed, yet for the sanity of the administrator the setting of policy should be centralized; if our hardworking administrator has to update dozens of machines in order to change the policies a little bit, someday one of them will get missed, and an intruder only needs one hole....

Further, by distributing the functionality, the network perimeter ceases to be a bottleneck, since local policy-enforcement entities only need to deal with a small fraction of the total traffic.

This model of firewall technology implies that some things need to be modified to enable this to work:

- Endpoint Authentication: new information element in setup message with authentication information. Various algorithms can be used, but signaling message flow restricts them (one message to, one message from). Verify release to avoid denial of service.
- Admission Control: Does the authenticated endpoint have permission to make the connection it requested?
- Connection Authentication: Make sure the data flowing across the connection is going where it is supposed to. In IP terms, make sure that if we establish a VC for a relatively innocuous connection to deliver ping packets, that the sender does not suddenly start sending packets to the Telnet daemon and try to log in. Without such authentication, the sender could just start sending TCP packets for port 23 (the default Telnet port) down the supposedly safe Ping VC, and when the packets are delivered to IP, they would be duly processed. This authentication also provides protection against wiretapping, where an adversary makes a physical connection to the wires of fibers, and against connection hijacking, where an adversary takes over an existing connection and masquerades as the already-authenticated user.

A periodic exchange of cryptographic information could provide such continuous authentication; perhaps after every AAL5 frame an OAM cell with a digital signature for the frame could be sent. If the signature doesn't match, appropriate action could be taken. Depending on the security policy, this could range from merely dropping the frame to setting off warning alarms in the security office.

Signaling must also interact with a secure audit system; an insecure audit is worse than useless, since all the audit information would become suspect when security is compromised, casting doubt on the very information needed to catch the interloper.

7.6 Summary

This chapter described how ATM networks can be managed. First, network management was defined, and then the command Internet management protocol SNMP was described.

The ATM Forum's Interim Local Management Interface (ILMI) provides ATM-specific management capabilities and uses much of the SNMP structure.

The IETF's Next Hop Router Protocol (NHRP) is still a work in progress, but allows hosts and routers to gain the information they need to make virtual connections that cut across large networks, to minimize the number of router hops to the destination.

Finally, we considered that bastion of defense popular with many installations, the firewall, and how ATM is both a blessing and a curse to firewall implementors.

IP Multicast

Multicast is the term for sending a packet to a group of hosts instead of to a single host. Normal "unicast" transmission involves sending a packet to a single destination and is so common that we rarely think of it in these terms. "Broadcast" is the practice of sending a packet to *all* hosts (in a limited area).

Multicast falls between these extremes. It is useful for building distributed pseudo-real-time applications such as videoconferencing and audioconferencing. However, its use is not restricted to these kinds of applications. Any application that involves sending copies of data to multiple places can benefit. For instance, one could distribute network routing tables to all routers in an enterprise, while not burdening all of the workstations with processing (and throwing away) all of the messages. There have even been proposals to use it for distributing Usenet News [Lidl 94].

The advantage to using multicast for this is that only one copy of the message needs to be sent in order for all recipients to get their copy, while any hosts on the network that don't want the data don't have to be bothered with it.

8.1 How Multicast Works

If a connection-oriented approach is used, then each sender will have a connection to each receiver. Right away, we have an N^2 problem.

But even worse than that, the sender has no idea what the actual layout of the network is. The sender sees the network (and its connections) as in Figure 8-1, when in fact the network may *really* look like Figure 8-2.

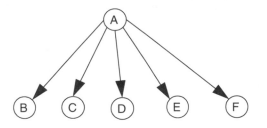

Figure 8-1. Naive view of connection-oriented network.

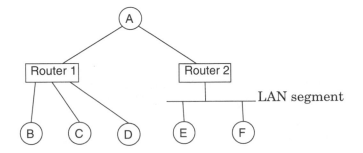

Figure 8-2. Actual network topology.

When A sends a packet to its leaves B through F, it sends a copy to each of its leaves, one over each connection that it has. Three copies of the packet traverse the link to Router 1, and two more copies go over the link to Router 2. Such duplication of traffic is clearly less than optimal. If we can arrange for the *routers* to duplicate the packets instead, we will greatly reduce traffic on the links to node A—and perhaps even the link from Router 2 to the LAN segment— since many LANs use a shared medium and one need not send duplicate traffic; instead, each host that is listening to the traffic will grab a copy of the packet as it whizzes past.

In fact, this is exactly how IP multicast works [Deering RFC 1112]. Class D addresses are reserved for "multicast groups." If a host wishes to receive a given transmission, it joins the group and sends a message to that effect to the multi-cast router, or *mrouter*, responsible for its network segment. The mrouter then "knows" that there is a recipient on that segment and starts sending (or contin-ues to send) packets for that multicast group to the host. The sender just sends its data out and its mrouter conspires with the others to arrange that all "inter-ested" receivers get it.

When a host starts sending on a multicast group, the mrouters flood the data to all their neighboring mrouters. When a packet for a given group comes in over a second link, then the mrouter sends a "prune" message back up that link, since it represents a longer path than the one it is already using to receive the data. Further, if an mrouter "knows" that there are no listeners downstream, it can send a prune message back up its primary link, saying in effect "Thanks, but no thanks! No one is listening so don't bother to send the data."

The protocol that hosts use to join and leave multicast groups is called the Internet Group Management Protocol (IGMP).

The mrouters use the Distance Vector Multicast Routing Protocol (DVMRP) [RFC 1075] to communicate with each other and perform the conspiring alluded to above.

When the host leaves the multicast group, it also sends a message to the mrouter. When no hosts on the network segment are members of the group, the mrouter can stop forwarding that group's packets altogether, avoiding clogging the segment with useless packets.

This distributed multicast routing scales quite well, as we can see in Section 8.2.

The problem of how to discover what is the address of a given group, is solved by assigning a "well-known" Class D address for "session announcements." Hosts can listen to these periodic announcements, keep a list of active sessions, and then join a session at any time.

Multicast programs use UDP instead of TCP. For one thing, the nature of most multicast streams is such that if a packet or two gets lost there is no disaster; perhaps a glitch in the audio or a part of a video frame doesn't get updated for another 30 msec.

But there's a more pressing reason. Remember that TCP uses acknowledgments to control the window—the amount that can be sent at any given time. If a sender has 200 receivers, which of the 200 ACKs that come back should it listen to? What does it do if one machine drops a packet but the rest don't? And finally, how does it even deal with 200 ACK packets all essentially arriving simultaneously?

No, UDP is better than TCP for these purposes and even can be used for "reliable" data transfer by layering on extra connections for dealing with dropped packets. At least one implementation of Usenet news distributed over multicast channels has been built [RFC1301].

8.2 The Mbone

The multicast backbone or Mbone was developed in March 1992 to carry an audio "mcast" of the San Diego IETF meeting. The initial deployment enabled the meeting to be seen and participated in by folks from 20 sites on three continents [Casner 1992].

Since that first small transmission, the Mbone has since grown to over 1000 sites worldwide and seen many kinds of mcasts, from the garage rock of Severe Tire Damage[1] to technical talks, NASA Space Shuttle missions, trade-show broadcasts and more. It has become common for technical conferences (especially Internet-related ones) to mcast portions of their meetings: Usenix, the IETF, Networld*Interop and BayLISA are just a few. Figure 8-3 shows a typical list of sessions.

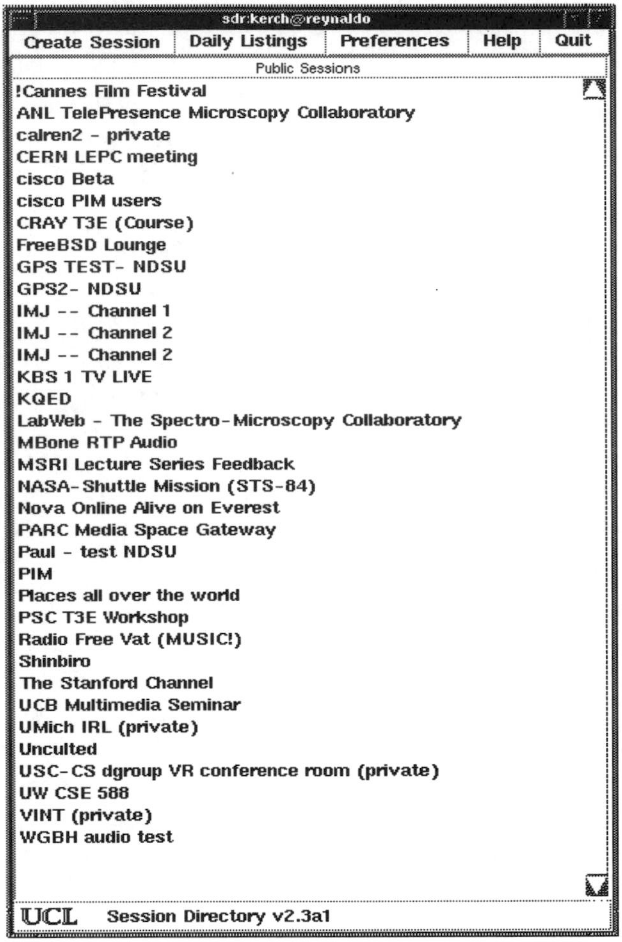

Figure 8-3. Multicast sessions on the Mbone.

---

[1] First live music broadcast on the Internet, see http://www.std.org for more info.

Some of these sessions can be quite popular. Figure 8-4 shows the members of a session watching the NASA Space Shuttle mcast on a Saturday afternoon. The famous Rolling Stones mcast had over 200 listeners as you can see at the Stones' web site: `http://www.stones.com`.

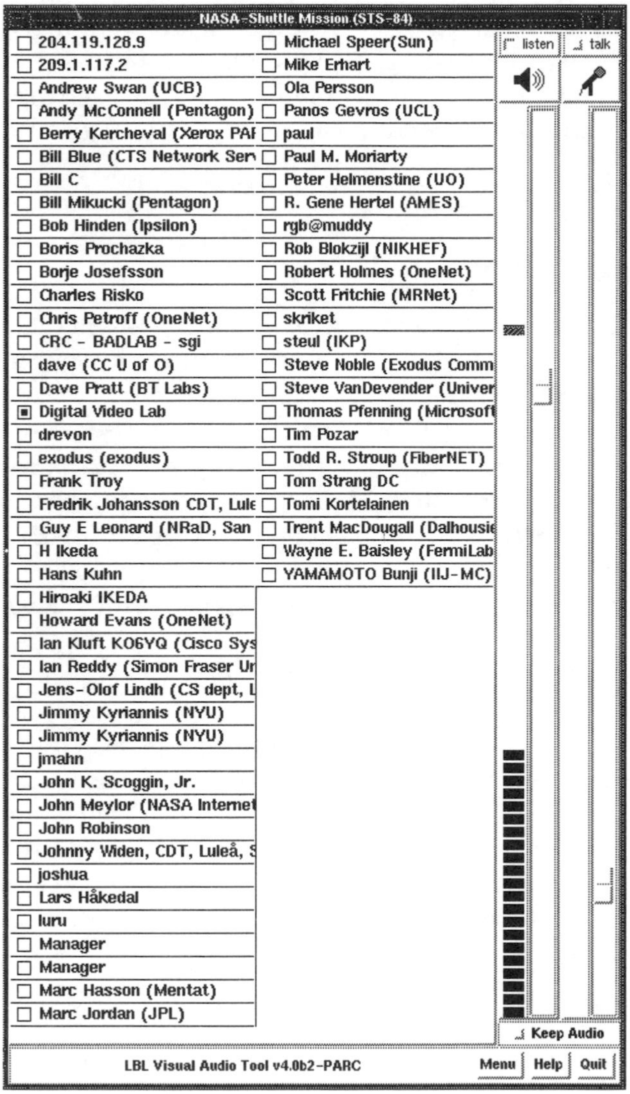

Figure 8-4. NASA Shuttle viewers as shown by the VAT tool.

Besides these public sessions, private sessions can be set up too. Most of the mbone programs provide the ability to encrypt the data with a key that is agreed upon in advance by the participants; this way, even if an outsider can intercept the data, it is useless without the key.

Since not all core routers have multicast functionality, the Mbone is built as a virtual network using *tunneling*. When a router needs to send a multicast packet to another router to which it is connected by a such a tunnel, it encapsulates the packet inside a unicast IP packet and sends it through the tunnel. The destination router unwraps the packet and drops the multicast packet into its local network (as well as forwarding it through any more tunnels it may have).

The current Mbone is maintained by volunteers who coordinate through a set of Internet mailing lists. Improved routing and transport algorithms are the subject of much active study. More information can be found at the WWW site `http://www.mbone.com`

8.3 Multicast Support in ATM

Support for multicast is built into the ATM specifications so that multipoint virtual circuits can be established, and many ATM switches have multicast support incorporated in their hardware.

Multicast is carried over virtual circuits that start at one place (called the *root node*) and end at several others (called *leaf nodes*). These are called *point-to-multipoint* circuits in contrast to the more usual *point-to-point* circuits. When a cell is transmitted from the starting point it is delivered to all of the destinations.

Most point-to-multipoint schemes do not allow nonzero bandwidth from the leaf nodes back to the root node, essentially making them one-way circuits. The reason for this is that the cells from several leaf nodes could get intermingled on their way to the root node, making separating out which cell belongs to which packet difficult (if not impossible).[2]

There are several ways of dealing with this problem. First of all, one could use AAL3/4 to carry the data and assign each leaf node a unique MID value to be used to demultiplex the cells at the root. This has the disadvantages that AAL3/4 has to be used, which is overly complex and cumbersome, and that there is no standardized way of assigning these MID values to the leaf nodes. Moreover, the 10-bit MID value would restrict the number of leaves to at most 1024, severely restricting scalability.

The next scheme uses a point-to-multipoint virtual path to carry the data, and each leaf is assigned a unique VCI within the path. This allows any AAL to be used, but still suffers from lack of standardized ways to distribute the VCI information.

Use of a multicast server, to which all multicast traffic is sent for redistribution to all leaves, works well, but the server becomes a performance bottleneck

---

[2] Well, one could take a burst of packets that fail to reassemble and (assuming AAL5) count the PTI bits to figure out how many packets there are, decode the trailers to find out how long each packet should be and then systematically shuffle the cells around until a good CRC is obtained, but we're talking about *practical* solutions.

and increases packet latency. In addition, the server is a single point of failure unless redundant multicast servers are used. Alas, redundant servers are not supported in current standards. This technique is used by the ATM Forum's LAN Emulation.

Finally, a "forest of trees" can be used; for N nodes we build N point-to-multipoint trees, each rooted in one sending node, with the N-1 other nodes as its leaves. This has good performance characteristics (there is no single-point bottleneck) and minimizes latency, but the bookkeeping involved is complex. A node joining or leaving a multicast group will cause a flurry of signaling messages. This technique is used in the IETF multicast proposals.

8.3.1 ATM Hardware Support

Hardware support for multicast can be (and is) provided by many different mechanisms. Here is a sampling of techniques.

In the Xerox PARC experimental "BADLAN" switch (Figure 8-5) multicast is supported by tagging a given VC as a multicast VC. Instead of going to an output port, cells from multicast VCs are routed to a "copynet," a small crossbar that causes duplicate cells to be deposited in the input ports of several ports. These cells are then routed to the output ports in the normal way, *without* multicast tags this time.

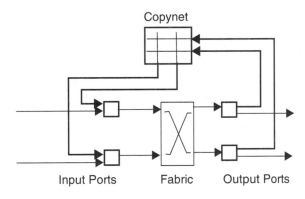

Figure 8-5. Xerox "BADLAN" copynet.

Fore Systems Forerunner® switches use a distributed shared-memory architecture. Each cell to be transmitted is placed in the shared memory with a "scorecard" attached, listing the ports that need to transmit the cell. If the cell is part of a multicast flow, then its scorecard will list all of the ports that flow should go to. As each port transmits the cell, it removes its identifier from the scorecard, and when the last port identifier is removed, the cell is deleted from the shared memory.

8.3.2 ATM Software Support

Using signaling based on UNI 3.1, a point-to-multipoint circuit is set up in the following way.

First, the node that is the sender creates a point-to-point circuit to the first leaf node. Once this circuit is established the root node can send "add party request" messages to cause additional leaf nodes to be added to the circuit.

The root node will eventually get "add party reply" messages from the network indicating whether the request succeeded (the leaf node was successfully added) or not. Since these replies contain identification of the leaf node in question, the root node can, if it is appropriate, issue multiple "add party requests" without waiting for the replies.

Leaf nodes can be dropped from the circuit at any time, either by the root node or at their own request.

Notice that the leaf node can drop out by itself but cannot add itself to a point-to-multipoint circuit. This style of addition used in UNI 3.1 is called "sender-initiated join" and leads to some problems when implementing IP multicast, as we will see in Section 8.4.

The bandwidth allowed from the leaf nodes back to the root must be zero, since if it were nonzero, the cells from packets from several leaf nodes could get intermingled as they traveled back to the root node, and packet reassembly would be impossible.

The newer version of the signaling document, UNI 4.0, adds support for "leaf-initiated join," whereby leaf nodes can join themselves to an existing point-to-multipoint virtual circuit.

8.4 IP Multicast Implementation for Classical IP

The document that describes the IETF scheme for implementing multicast on ATM networks is RFC 2022 [Armitage 1996]. It's designed to work with RFC1577's Classical IP and UNI signaling 3.1.

RFC 2022 describes two schemes for implementing multicast; one using a mesh of multicast virtual circuits, the other using a multicast server. Both techniques have pluses and minuses as we shall see.

The main problem with implementing IP multicast over ATM is similar to the ATM ARP problem in Classical IP. Given a Class D multicast group address you wish to join, how do you find out the ATM address to which you send your join request? Remember that only the root of a point-to-multipoint circuit can add a leaf; it is necessary to figure out who the root is and ask it to add you.

Actually, it's worse. If there are many senders in a session, you have to figure out the roots of *all* senders and ask *all* of them to add you.

8.4.1 MARS Needs Packets!

A Multicast Address Resolution Server (MARS) is the answer. The MARS is a repository of information about who belongs to what multicast group. It stores the multicast group identifiers (in the case of IP multicast, these are the Class D IP addresses)[3] along with a list of the ATM addresses of the group members.

8.4.2 Multicast Clusters

The MARS manages a *cluster* of ATM end points. The cluster is just the group of end points that want to use the same MARS to deal with this multicast bookkeeping.

Due to lack of knowledge, and especially experience about what would happen otherwise, a cluster is required to be a subset of a unicast logical IP subnet (LIS). So while there can be multiple multicast clusters in a single LIS, one may not span multiple LISs. Instead, IP multicast routers must be used to interconnect clusters on different LISs.

The nodes in a cluster must be configured with the ATM address of the MARS for that cluster. This is not as onerous as it sounds; it's just another entry in the checklist for installing a new machine.[4]

8.4.3 MARS Messages

All MARS messages are required to be encapsulated using LLC/SNAP as described in Section 5.3 and must use an OUI of 0x00-00-5E (IANA) and a protocol identifier of 0x00-03, which identifies the datagram as a MARS message.

The MARS message is composed of four parts:

1. header,
2. required fields,
3. addresses, and
4. additional data.

The header has a fixed length of 20 bytes. This header carries information about which MARS operation this message represents, the address family and length and type of addresses (always ATM, but left configurable for future expansion), protocol type (so it can support more than just IP Multicast), and a checksum.

---

[3] The author of this RFC, and the working group members, try hard not to preclude the use of their work by protocols other than IP.

[4] Although changing the MARS address for all the hosts in a large cluster could be very painful; when moving a MARS to a new host it may be simpler to change the ATM address of the new MARS host to match what everyone else thinks it should be.

The protocol field of the MARS message is encoded with a 16-bit type and a 40-bit SNAP extension. The type field identifies the family of protocol types; a value of 0x0080 indicates SNAP encoded extensions (in the SNAP field, of course) and is considered the "long form" of the protocol identifier. Otherwise the SNAP field is ignored and the type field is assumed to be an Ethertype and is called the "short-form PID."

8.4.4 Signaling Support

MARS Multicast assumes that hosts can use the following signaling functions:

- **CALL**—Establishes a unicast VC to an address.
- **MULTI_RQ**—Establishes multicast VC to an address.
- **MULTI_ADD**—Adds a new leaf node to previously established VC.
- **MULTI_DROP**—Removes a leaf node from established VC.
- **RELEASE**—Releases a unicast VC or all of the leaves of a multicast VC.

8.4.5 Joining and Leaving the Cluster

A host becomes a member of the cluster when it registers with the MARS. The host establishes a point-to-point connection to the MARS and sends a MARS_JOIN message with the `register` bit set, including its ATM address in the message.

The MARS adds the host to a point-to-multipoint circuit it maintains called the *ClusterControlVC*, and allocates a 16-bit Cluster Member ID (CMI) for the host. The CMI is returned to the host in the acknowledging MARS_JOIN message.

To leave a cluster, the host may send a MARS_LEAVE message, whereupon the MARS will drop the host from the ClusterControlVC, free the CMI, and forget about the host entirely.

8.4.6 Joining a Group

To join a multicast group, the host first sends a MARS_JOIN message to the MARS. The MARS propagates the MARS_JOIN messages to the members of the group so that they can add the host to their transmit VCs as a leaf.

If it wishes to not just listen, but send data, then the host needs to establish a VC so that it can transmit to the group, so it needs a set of ATM addresses of the other members of the group. To learn this it sends a MARS_REQUEST with the Class D IP address of the multicast group in question. The MARS will reply with either a MARS_NAK, if there is no such group (or at least, the MARS doesn't know of such a group) or a series of MARS_MULTI addresses containing the ATM addresses of all the members of the group.

Now the host creates a multipoint VC to the first address with a MULTI_RQ signaling message, and when that is established, adds the rest of the leaves with MULTI_ADD.

Now the host can listen for MARS_JOIN and MARS_LEAVE messages from the MARS so as to keep the list of its leaves current, adding and dropping them as they leave or join the session.

8.4.7 Leaving a Group

To leave a group, the host sends a MARS_LEAVE message to the MARS that says "so long and thanks for all the bits." This is propagated to all other group members (like the MARS_JOIN was) and the other group members drop the host from their VCs. Likewise, the host RELEASEs its own multipoint VC and is no longer a group member.

8.4.8 Backup MARS

Having a single server to deal with the address resolutions leads to a vulnerability: If the MARS crashes, no more multicast group changes can be made. To alleviate this, hosts can keep a table of backup MARSs and switch to one when it detects that the original MARS is unreachable. Events that can cause this change are:

- failure to connect to the MARS;
- failure of a MARS_REQUEST, MARS_JOIN, or MARS_LEAVE message; or
- failure to receive a list of alternate MARSs for 4 min.

This last event means that the host has missed the list of backup MARS addresses that the MARS periodically broadcasts, and that the MARS is probably dead.

8.4.9 Extended Encapsulation

So that hosts can detect their own packets coming back from a multicast server, an extended encapsulation format is required. The extra bits are used to carry a copy of the sending host's CMI and the layer three protocol id in a header that is stuffed between the LLC/SNAP header and the original packet. Type 1 encapsulation is required to be sent, Type 2 must not be sent, and either must be received. The purpose of Type 2 extended encapsulation is to permit future research on direct ATM multicast connections past cluster boundaries; a larger 8-byte source ID field is provided

The "regular" or Type 1 encapsulation comes in two flavors. First, if the protocol in use has a short-form representation, the short-form encapsulation can be used. Otherwise the long form, with the long form of the protocol ID, has to be used (Figure 8-6).

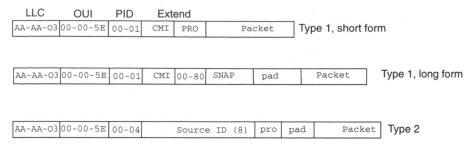

Figure 8-6. MARS extended encapsulations.

8.5 Multicast Implementation for LANE

Multicast on LAN emulation systems is pretty simple, but relies on hiding the complexity in the ability to establish signaled point-to-multipoint virtual circuits.

When a LAN Emulation Client (LEC) wants to send a multicast packet, it sends it over its previously established Multicast-Send VC to the Broadcast and Unknown Server (BUS). The server then sends it back out on the Multicast-Forward VC and all the LECs receive the packet (see Figure 6-2). Remember from Chapter 6 that the LEC was able to determine the ATM address of the BUS by using ARP to resolve the broadcast address.

This way of sending multicast packets allows the emulated LAN to behave like a traditional shared-medium LAN; all stations get a crack at receiving the packet. Disadvantages are that every station *has* to look at the packet and decide whether to discard it or accept it; this can be inefficient. Also, aggregate multicast bandwidth on the emulated LAN is restricted to that of one VC or to how much the BUS can handle. Where using independent multipoint VCs allows multiple noninterfering flows, the server-based multicast approach introduces a bottleneck at the server.

Further, the switches in the ELAN must support point-to-multipoint signaling for this approach to work. Not all commercial switches do, but this lack is becoming less common as the products mature.

8.6 Summary

In this chapter we saw how multicast transmission of packets works and a sampling of the things it is useful for. The Mbone multicast backbone network was described.

Next came a sampling of techniques used by ATM switches to implement multicast transmission.

Finally, descriptions of the ATM Forum's LAN Emulation approach to multicast and the IETF's "MARS" complete the chapter.

CHAPTER 9

Traffic Management

Unlike traditional forms of networking, ATM provides the capability to manage the network traffic. This means allocating bandwidth to different connections in such a way that each gets its "fair share," whatever the definition of "fair" happens to be. Connections that need constant bandwidth, low-latency connections are able to request and get what is needed. Since some ATM networks are public, the idea that "you get what you pay for" is taking hold: pay more and get more bandwidth, pay less and get your cells through only if there's leftover room in the data stream.

Until recently the Internet was, for the most part, a friendly cooperative community, and widespread deployment of BSD Unix (and the networking code derived from it) meant that reasonable congestion-control algorithms were in place. With recent explosive growth, the number of "bad guys" has increased (along with "good guys," of course), and more implementations of TCP/IP are out there, not all of which are perfectly implemented.

9.1 Traffic Classes

Several classes of traffic have been defined for ATM data flows so that they can be treated separately.

Constant Bit Rate (CBR)—"Constant Bit Rate" traffic is just that, the number of bits of data that flow per second varies very little for the duration of the connection. The actual bit rate used is specified at the time the connection is set up. If the actual amount of data exceeds this amount it is likely to be discarded.

CBR traffic is usually sensitive to delays; that is, if the data arrives late, it may as well not arrive at all. It is also often sensitive to cell-delay variation. The time between cells is expected to remain nearly constant, as some applications derive their timing from cell arrivals.

An example of a CBR data flow might be an uncompressed video stream; the number of bits per video frame and the number of frames per second can be predicted accurately.

Variable Bit Rate (VBR)—VBR traffic is similar to CBR, but the amount of data flowing at any instant can vary somewhat. The flow is characterized by an average bit rate and a peak rate, saying, in essence, "I'll usually send this much (average rate), but I might send as much as this (peak rate) once in a while." This allows occasional bursts of data to be carried without loss as long as the average rate isn't exceeded over a long span of time. VBR traffic can be sub-divided into "real-time" and "non-real-time" traffic. Real-time VBR traffic is also sensitive to delays, while non-real-time VBR traffic is more tolerant of delay.

An example of real-time VBR traffic is compressed video. The number of frames per second is known, and the average size of a frame can be well-characterized, but the exact amount any given frame can be compressed is unpredictable, since, for example, an all-black video frame found between scenes can be compressed to a very tiny size, while a complex scene cannot be compressed as hard without losing detail.

Unspecified Bit Rate (UBR)—UBR is the class that most "traditional" Internet traffic would fall into. Remember that in the Internet, packet delivery is not guaranteed; the best that the network will promise is to try hard to get your data to its destination. This is quite acceptable for many types of Internet traffic. You won't really care if your mail gets to me in five minutes or six, when I probably won't answer it until tomorrow anyway.

UBR is the ATM equivalent of the Internet "Best Effort" traffic. Any cells waiting to be sent on UBR connections have to wait until there is free bandwidth available that is not being used by CBR or VBR traffic.

Available Bit Rate (ABR)—ABR is similar to UBR, but has been made a more "respected" class by the ATM Forum—it is no longer like the UBR's "everything that didn't fit another class." ABR connections can have a guaranteed minimum cell rate (MCR), and excess traffic up to a specified peak cell rate (PCR) is admitted to the network on a "space available" basis. This allows an upper bound on the time a given transfer will take, which makes many people more comfortable with its unpredictability. The MCR can be set to zero, in which case all of the data for a given connection must be flow-controlled.

ABR also specifies flow-control mechanisms to prevent overloading links and wasting bandwidth by retransmitting lost data. Among the possible flow-control methods is a closed-loop feedback method that uses special out-of-band Resource Management (RM) cells to convey the feedback information to the sender.

ABR is suitable for applications that have only an approximate bandwidth requirement; bulk data with a bound on transfer times (such as stock market trading updates) might use it.

Figure 9-1 shows how a combination of CBR, VBR, and ABR traffic can fully utilize a network link over time. Note that the ABR traffic takes up whatever is "left over" after the CBR and VBR traffic is dealt with.

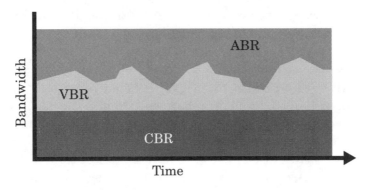

Figure 9-1.   ATM traffic classes.

9.2 How Can Traffic Be Degraded?

Any kind of network traffic is subject to errors, whether from electromagnetic noise degrading the signals, dirty connections reducing signals to marginal levels, or any of a host of other possibilities. However, even assuming that the network equipment is working without errors, factors in the data stream can still cause problems.

There are two principal ways that traffic flows can be degraded: cell loss and cell delays.

First, cells can be lost due to congestion. If incoming streams that all need to go out on a single link exceed the link capacity, then some of the cells must be dropped. Sure, they can be buffered and sent later when the pressure eases off, but if the pressure *doesn't* ease off, then eventually some *will* be dropped because no switches ever made have infinite buffering. Even the biggest bucket will eventually fill up.

Secondly, cells may be delayed enough so that their utility is impaired. Getting frame 37 of a video stream when it's time to show frame 38 doesn't help a bit. It actually hurts, since now the real frame 38 is delayed behind the now-useless frame 37.

The same congestion that fills up the buffers can cause cells to be delayed, and machines that are "poor network neighbors" can send long bursts of packets, fill up the buffers, and trap high-priority (but more polite) traffic behind it. (This will be discussed further in the next section.)

9.3 Traffic Control

9.3.1 Requirements

Before we discuss schemes to control ATM traffic, it's worthwhile to consider what the desirable properties of a good scheme would be.

First of all, an ideal traffic-control scheme should be *fair*, whatever that means. Everyone agrees that fairness is a good thing, but it's hard to pin down.

Clearly, all of the users of the network should be able to get their data through the network in a reasonable time. Depending on the needs of the traffic, they can select one of the appropriate traffic classes that will ensure that the data arrive intact and in time.

If all of the classes of traffic carry the same price, or no price, there is a potential for problems, which leads to a small digression.

In medieval times, villages often had a field called the "commons" where anyone could graze their cattle. As long as everyone was sensible about things this worked well, but some bright and unscrupulous person eventually figured out that the "cost" to him was the same if he grazed one cow or 20, so why not graze more? Other people saw this and decided to graze more cattle too, and eventually the poor overgrazed commons was destroyed, every vestige of grass swallowed by hungry cattle, and the soil trampled into a muddy wreck. This phenomenon is called "the Tragedy of the Commons."

In networking, the bandwidth available is the "commons," we users of the net are the peasants and our packets are the cattle. If there is no incentive to be frugal with bandwidth, some folks will take as much as they can get, to the detriment of other users.

So, to get back to the topic at hand, one type of fairness would be to ensure that all users' packets get through the network with about equal performance. An added feature might be to allow those that really need specific performance to get it by paying for it. This is considered antithetical to the spirit of the Internet by some partisans, but others argue that it's the only way to avoid the Tragedy of the Commons.

The next desired characteristic of a good traffic-control scheme is that is be *robust*. That is, it should continue to work well in the face of stresses.

The scheme should be resistant to external forces; if the legendary backhoe severs a fiber link in Montana, the network may be partitioned into west and east halves, but each half should continue to work. If a defective SONET regenerator inserts a burst of random noise, the members of the net ought to be able to recover and not become terminally confused.

Further, the scheme should be able to tolerate "poor citizens"; the node that sends traffic in excess of their agreed limit should not profit from this, nor should other nodes' traffic be impaired.

Until recently the Internet was, for the most part, a friendly cooperative community, but widespread deployment of millions of hosts means that, unfortunately, some unscrupulous types will slip in and the network must be prepared to deal with them.

There are also two facets to the control of traffic: *prevention* and *reaction*. Prevention aims to avoid congestion and excess delay by only allowing traffic that will have acceptable characteristics; reaction deals with what to do after congestion occurs.

Prevention can take several forms:

- *Admission*: Only accept connections with characteristics that can be handled by the network. Reject connections that ask for excessive resources or that will overload part of the network.
- *Policing*: When a host sets up a connection with the promise that the traffic will never exceed a certain rate, keep track of the actual rate; if it goes over the agreed limit, drop the cells.

Shaping is done by the sender of the traffic. When the connection was established, a "contract" between the sender and the network was made. The sender must abide by this contract. If the promise was to send 5000 cells per second, it must not send 6000.

Most "recent" ATM interface cards have built-in hardware support for traffic shaping. These typically can be set to send cells belonging to a certain connection at a specified rate.

Policing is the enforcement arm of traffic control. It is implemented in switches, amounting to a policy about what to do with cells in excess of the agreed rate and a mechanism for implementing the policy.

End stations don't usually have policing functions, since a sender has the shaping mechanisms, and if the traffic makes it intact to a receiver, well that's fine! Why throw away perfectly good data that have made it safe to their destination?

Several things can be done with cells that exceed the agreed traffic parameters, and choosing which is an administrative decision. The choices include:

- Just drop the excess cells. This is simple, but leads to packets arriving at their destinations with cells missing; transporting information that has no hope of being useful is a waste.

- Drop the excess cells and all of the cells in the packets that they belong to. This is substantially more complicated to implement since the switch has to keep track of which packets are flowing through on which VCs.

- If the total bandwidth is not exceeded, mark the excess cells with CLP = 1. Setting the Cell-Loss Priority bit in the cell header allows the next switch along to drop these cells if it is congested, since they were "illegal" in the first place, but in the absence of congestion they can go on through.

Whichever scheme is used, it's important to communicate it to the users. As an example, when conducting the trials in BAGNet [Laubach 94, Johnston 94] we experienced mysterious cell loss, even though we had specified the maximum available bandwidth for all of our virtual circuits. As reported in [Berc 95], the problem was traced to the fact that for the particular ATM switches used in the BAGNet backbone, specifying 140 Mbits (the maximum effective throughput on an OC-3, after overhead) is very different from specifying "no limit." In the latter case, the cells just stream through the switch without problems, but if *any* limit is specified, the cells have to pass through a separate hardware policing unit to ensure that they meet the agreed limits, and the policing unit is slower. It was unable to process large IP packets that were sent out as long bursts of back-to-back cells.

The limit was installed due to a misunderstanding between the provider of the backbone service and the BAGNet representative asking for the virtual circuits to be established. Once the limit was removed everything behaved properly and no more cells were lost.

9.3.2 Congestion Control Schemes

There are two aspects to proposed congestion control schemes that are mostly independent of each other. First there's the control algorithm itself, and next there's the range over which the algorithm is applied. [Yang 95] presents a more complete taxonomy of schemes; I'm just hitting the high points.

9.3.3 Algorithms

Two main control algorithms have been proposed for controlling ATM traffic. One is called a "credit-based" scheme. The receiver grants a token of some kind to the sender, which allows it to send some number of cells, after which it must wait for another token. TCP flow control is a credit scheme; a window update amounts to credit to send a given number of bytes.

As we will see in Chapter 10, as link speeds and link delays become large, the amount of buffering (and therefore, the amount of credit extended to the sender) needs to grow in order to extract the best performance from the link.

The other principal traffic control method is a "rate-based" scheme. Instead of transmitting cells in response to credits, an explicit permitted rate is given to each sender; the sum of the rates of all senders on a given link should not exceed the link capacity, of course.

The usual model of the rate-control mechanism is of a "leaky bucket" shown in Figure 9-2. The leak is the output and is carefully sized to permit through exactly the desired number of cells per second. The bucket itself is the buffer in which cells are stored. As long as the bucket doesn't fill up, the input cell rate can vary quite a bit, and the output will be controlled to fit the parameters of the QoS specified. If the bucket fills up—the cell buffers overflow—then some cells will be lost.

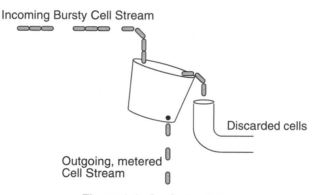

Figure 9-2. Leaky bucket.

This works quite well if each virtual circuit has its own bucket. Imagine for a moment that we have only one bucket for a link, and that we have two connections sharing the link. One is a high bit rate, delay-sensitive video stream, and the other is a bursty TCP stream. Most of the time things will work pretty well; the two streams get mingled in the bucket but the cells will get out in time. (Since each stream is labeled with a distinct VCI and VPI, the data can be sorted out at the destination.)

Now, the TCP stream suddenly gets very active and sends a lot of cells all at once. Perhaps the bucket doesn't actually fill up and overflow, but the delay-sensitive video cells that come in after this burst get put behind this large mass of cells. The video stream cells get unacceptably delayed even though there is no cell loss. This is another example of the *head-of-line blocking* that we saw in Section 4.3.3.

Having per-VC queuing enables this problem to be eliminated, at a cost of added complexity and expense in building an ATM switch. Early switches did not support this—we were happy to get switches that worked at all in 1992—but some of the more modern designs do.

What they wind up with is a set of buffers, whether individual (which limits the number of simultaneous rate-controlled VCs) or shared out of a big buffer pool (which makes implementation more complicated, since you have to keep track of which bit of the buffer belongs to which VC, and how much it can use, and so on).

Each buffer accumulates cells and, when according to the parameters for this VC, it's time to send a cell, it makes the cell available in the output. The bit of hardware that does the actual sending of cells will then take the available cells in turn from each buffer that is ready.

Algorithm range

These traffic-control algorithms can be applied over different ranges. Again, two main choices dominate: *end-to-end* or *hop-by-hop*. See Figure 9-3.

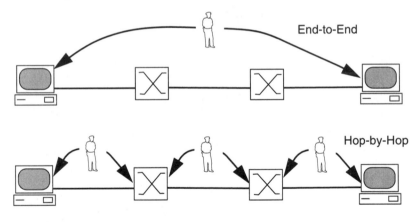

Figure 9-3. Traffic control ranges.

"End-to-end" means that the algorithm is applied over the entire length of the connection, and only the endpoints participate, with TCP large buffers.

"Hop-by-hop" means that the algorithm is applied over each link in the connection independently.

There has been a great deal of controversy over which is "best," for whatever interpretation of "best" one chooses. For large networks, end-to-end requires large buffers to avoid packet loss, since once congestion is detected the "stop sending" feedback must propagate all the way from the receiver to the sender, and a large amount of data could be "in flight" at the time. Some authors claim that TCP, even with slow-start, exhibits start-up oscillations of throughput that are detrimental to the overall health of the network.

Hop-by-hop, on the other hand, requires only enough buffering to handle the data in flight on a single link, but requires per-VC queueing of cells to be effective.

9.4 RSVP

The Resource ReSerVation Protocol (RSVP)[1] is a scheme that operates at the IP layer to, well, reserve resources for "flows" of packets, both unicast and multicast as well. RSVP is being developed by the IETF and at this writing is still in the "Internet Draft" stage and therefore must be considered a "work in progress."

RSVP is designed to work with both IPv4, the current Internet standard, and with IPv6. It is not a routing protocol, but works with existing (and future) routing protocols to provide reservations. It is intended that RSVP be scalable, that it be able to deal with both large flows and large numbers of flows.

RSVP only deals with flows in one direction, from some sender to one or more receivers (Figure 9-4). Thus, if we are making a unidirectional connection, the sender may connect to the receiver and the receiver will then send back an RSVP request along the path from here to there. The message travels along the path from hop to hop, and each router or other device in the path gets to decide if this reservation is acceptable.

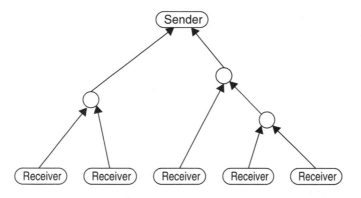

Figure 9-4. RSVP message flow.

If we have a multicast tree, though, it's a little more complicated. In this case, each receiver sends an RSVP request, and the intermediate nodes aggregate the resources needed and pass the requests along.

---

[1] Yes, it is supposed to be capitalized that way. "RSVP" is *usually* the abbreviation for the French "rêpondez s'il vous plait", or "please reply," and is the only example of the use of French subjunctives I can reliably remember.

RSVP is organized in two main parts (Figure 9-5). First is the RSVP part itself that allocates resources based on requests from receivers. This has two parts itself: admission control, that decides whether there are sufficient free resources to accept this request, and policy control, which decides whether this request should be allowed based on local policy. Some sites might want to give preference to local traffic, for instance, or set a limit on how much bandwidth an outsider can reserve.

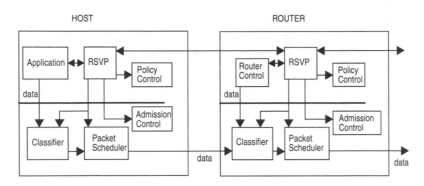

Figure 9-5. RSVP architecture (after [Braden97]).

The second part is the traffic control, which consists of a packet classifier and a packet scheduler. The classifier determines which class a given packet belongs to, and the scheduler arranges that the packets are transmitted in time to meet the promised QoS.

So far the designers of RSVP have completed Internet Drafts describing the protocol and built a prototype implementation to prove that it can work. Many Internet vendors are building RSVP or RSVP-like products, so there is a great deal of interest, not to say pressure to get things done! Information on current status (almost certainly changed by the time you read this) can be found on the World Wide Web at the RSVP Home Page, http://www.isi.edu/div7/rsvp/

9.5 Self-Similar Traffic

In the last few years a very interesting topic has been "What is the traffic on real networks like?" Some folks have put monitoring equipment on networks and captured data to answer this question, instead of relying on mathematical models to do their work.

Before we get into that let's look at some very basic theory of queuing systems. This will allow us to see why simple mathematical models are both attractive and dangerous.

Yes, there are some equations ahead but don't worry: I put them in mostly to show off so you don't need to understand them fully to follow the arguments.

9.5.1 Queueing Theory and Poisson Models

The basic idea of queuing theory is that there is a *server*, that does a task. Things *arrive* to have the task done to them, but since the server can only work on one task at a time, sometimes they have to wait in a *queue* (Figure 9-6). Mathematicians have developed ways for describing and reasoning about this situation and other similar ones. There may be multiple queues or multiple servers. There may be things that need several things done, perhaps in some order, perhaps not. All of the different combinations lead to different and interesting (if you're a mathematician) results.

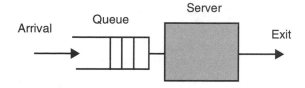

Figure 9-6. Queueing model.

Questions that queuing theory can answer are, given the characteristics of arrivals and server performance:

- How long will the queue get?
- What is the probability the queue will ever be N items long?
- What is the average time an item will wait in the queue?
- What is the maximum time an item will wait?

The application to computer or telephone networks is straightforward.[2] The items arriving are packets or cells, the queue is some kind of buffer, and the server is a switch, router, or other network device.

The main characteristic of the arrival of these items is time between successive arrivals. Since ATM cells are of fixed length, the size of the item is not a factor.

Often studies of theoretical network behavior are done assuming that arrival times obey a *Poisson Distribution* [Feller 1950]; that is

$$p(k;\lambda) = e^{-\lambda}\frac{\lambda^k}{k!}$$

---

[2] And pretty ancient by Internet standards; possibly the first paper applying queueing theory to telephone networks was C. Palm's "Intesitätsschwankungen im Fernsprachverkehr", *Ericsson Technics*, V. **44** (1943) pp 1–189.

where p the probability that k successes will occur in an experiment characterized by the parameter λ. In networking terms, λ is usually related to the average
interpacket delay, and "k successes" means k packets arrive in time t.

Mathematically inclined readers who haven't already skipped to the next
section will be rewarded with the observation that if you form the sum of this
equation for $k = 0, 1, 2, \ldots$ you get

$$\sum_0^\infty p(k;\lambda) = e^{-\lambda}\left(\frac{\lambda^0}{0!} + \frac{\lambda^1}{1!} + \frac{\lambda^2}{2!} + \ldots\right)$$

which is, on the right side, $e^{-\lambda}$ times the Taylor series for e^λ, the product, of
course, being 1; thus the sum of all the possible probabilities is 1, as we expect.
(Remember that a probability of 0 means something is impossible; 1 means it is
certain to occur; the probability that a fair coin-toss will come up heads is 0.5 and
so on.) In other words, if you add up the probabilities of all of the different things
that can happen, you discover that it is certain that *one* of them will happen.
This helps us believe the equations are correct, since if all of the probabilities
added to something else we'd know *something* was wrong.

9.5.2 Theoretical Versus Measured Traffic Characteristics

Lots of simulators and theoretical models use these Poisson models. From a
researcher's point of view they are quite attractive, since the mathematics are easy
to deal with, and it's easy to simulate Poisson processes with computer programs.

The problem is that real network traffic isn't like that. Poisson models
assume that the events in question are independent events. In any given time
segment, it's just as likely that a packet will arrive as in any other time segment.
In a sense, no event "knows" anything about any other event.

Careful measurement of real traffic on production networks has revealed
that network packet arrival times are in fact highly interdependent and bursty.
[Paxson 94] and [Leland 94] shows that for data traffic on Ethernets, while TCP
connection *establishments* follow Poisson statistics in arriving at hosts, the *traffic* on the links does not.

Subsequent work has demonstrated that this holds true for other network
media—ATM in particular—and for WAN traffic as well as LAN.

Currently researchers are working hard to figure out what this means for
traffic algorithms; interesting results should appear soon.

9.5.3 Implications for Control

Where Poisson-based modeling suggests that merely increasing buffer sizes
will reduce the packet drop rate, thus improving the overall network perfor-

mance, [Fowler 91] suggests that with traffic that is bursty at unpredictable time scales—exactly what Paxson and others found to be the case—the packet loss rate can increase dramatically with just a small increase in traffic. [Clark 92] shows that connection admission based on current measurements of actual traffic can lead to better bandwidth utilization than strict Poisson-model-based admission policies.

These and other theoretical papers predict that if traffic is bursty and unpredictable, then the Poisson models will not fit well, and the recent measurement papers show that traffic is indeed bursty and unpredictable.

9.6 Summary

In this chapter, the various ATM traffic classes were presented. The basic ideas of traffic management were laid out and characteristics of good control schemes was explored.

Finally, we looked at RSVP, the IETF scheme for resource reservation in the Internet, and at why mathematically "easy" network models didn't fit the measured characteristics of real network traffic.

Making It Go Fast

I hooked up to an OC-3 and don't get 155 Mbits! Why? What's wrong?

Often when people hook up an ATM network for the first time they get disappointingly slow performance. This chapter explains some of the reasons why ATM might not produce the kind of performance you expect, and what you can do about it.

A reasonable set of tune-up steps would be:

1. Figure out what kind of performance you expect from your system.
2. Measure the current performance.
3. Determine why performance is poor and fix it.
4. Measure again to make sure it is fixed.
5. If it's still not fast enough, go to step 3 and repeat.

The first step is very important. Regardless of what the salesman said, there aren't very many computers and ATM host cards that can source enough data to saturate an OC-3 link and still get useful work done. It's even a little harder for a machine to *accept* that much data and still do anything at all interesting. It can be done, but the equipment has to be chosen carefully. (And it *is* getting easier to find than it was a few years ago.)

10.1 What Does "Slow" Mean, or, How to Measure TCP Performance

If you are trying to tune a network, it is very important to be able to measure the performance of a link and to take notes of everything you do and the measurements before and after.

If you don't do this, you can't really tell if you have made things better or worse. This is the kind of thing people mean when they say, "If you can't measure it, it isn't science."

Therefore, find some tools to measure the aspect of performance you're interested in and use it consistently as you track down what's making your net slow.

Two popular (and free!) software tools are `netperf` and `ttcp`. See Appendix D for ways to get them.

10.1.1 ttcp

`ttcp` stands for "test TCP." It was originally written by Mike Muus of the U.S. Army's Ballistic Research Laboratory (BRL), which is now called the Army Research Lab (ARL), and by Terry Slattery, then at the U.S. Naval Academy.

`ttcp` is a program with a lot of options, but its basic operation is simple. To test the performance between two computers a copy of `ttcp` is run on one in "receive mode" and on the other in "transmit mode." The transmitting `ttcp` creates a connection to the receiving one, sends a lot of data to it as fast as it can, closes the connection, and then both sides figure out the data rate from how long it took and how much data were sent (or received).

There are many options. You ask for ttcp to itself generate the data to be sent, thus measuring performance from the sender's memory system to that of the receiver, or you can have it send "real" data from files you specify,[1] allowing one to use it to transfer files.

The size of buffers used to transmit, the number of them transmitted, and the amount of socket buffering to use can all be controlled, as can the format of the results.

Data can even be sent using UDP instead of TCP. Since UDP does not have flow control or guarantee delivery, results indicate the amount of data dropped between the sender and receiver. It's not uncommon to find that systems can send data faster than they can be received.

---

[1] For Unix wizards, it uses stdin and stdout.

`ttcp` is quite useful in debugging performance problems. It's a small, simple, portable program that doesn't use much in the way of fancy operating-system features, so it's easy to run on just about any kind of computer that supports TCP/IP with some kind of socket-like interface to it.

10.1.2 netperf

`netperf` is a similar program written at Hewlett-Packard's Information Networks Division by Rick Jones, Karen Choy, Dave Shield, and quite a few others.

The basic operation is similar to `ttcp`: `netperf` sends data from one machine to another and times how long it takes, but it has some additional features.

When installed according to the instructions, a `netperf` server runs on each machine to participate in the tests, and the `netperf` client program can connect to any of them and run tests. This means that one can make tests to remote machines without having to log in to them to run the receiver commands.

Besides just bulk-data transfers, `netperf` can run request/response tests wherein the client sends requests to the server, which then replies. This simulates transactions such as the World Wide Web's HTTP protocol.

Besides TCP sockets, `netperf` can handle several other types of network streams, including DLPI, Unix domain sockets, and the Fore Systems native ATM API.

While `netperf` has more features than `ttcp`, it is also more dependent on Unix features (and harder to port to non-Unix systems). Its requirement of root access to enable proper installation can be a problem in cases where you want to measure the performance to a remote machine to which you don't have the root password; luckily you can still run the server manually, but then you need a shell account on the remote machine (or a cooperative person resident over there).

10.2 Why It Is Slow

The next thing to do to make a network go fast is to figure out *why* it is slow. There are several factors that can affect things, from the hardware to the software to the protocols themselves. Taking a good look at all the pieces and tuning them up can reap big benefits in throughput.

10.2.1 Protocol Overhead

One of the things that can eat up your machine without getting much benefit is *protocol overhead*. If an OC-3 SONET link is blasting packets at you at 155 Mbit/sec, you are flat going to get a lot more packets than a fully loaded Ethernet can deliver.

Each packet a computer receives must be processed. The network card and protocol stack must do several things for each packet:

1. verify that it's for this computer,
2. verify the checksums and CRCs,
3. decide what protocol it's for, and
4. deliver it to that protocol.

Each of these takes time, and if the protocol stack is not efficient about it, maximum performance will not occur.

10.2.2 Machine Architectures

Some machines are just not built for high-speed data communication. As an example, the data-moving performance of the IBM-PC's ISA bus is widely considered to be, on a clear day with a following wind, pathetic.

The choice of the payload size in the ATM cell turns out to be a problem here. Almost all computer buses transfer data in units of a power of two, yet the payload of a cell is 48 bytes, or 32 + 16. If a system does 32-byte bus transfers, then when the ATM interface card transfers the data into host memory as it reassembles the packet, one-half of a transfer is going to be wasted. In some cases, the 16-byte transfer may even take longer than the 32-byte transfer, since the bus has been optimized for large transfers, such as from disk.

10.2.3 Long Fat Pipes

One important thing to remember in dealing with high-performance telecommunication is this important fact:

The speed of light stays the same.

This *seems* perfectly obvious, but think for a minute. Let's say you have two computers, one in, say, Palo Alto, California and one in Sydney, Australia (Table 10-1). The great circle distance between them is 11942.810 kms.[2] Let's use 12,000 in our calculation to make it easier, and to allow that we probably cannot get a wire or fiber laid straight along the great circle route anyway.

Remembering that the speed of light is close to three hundred million kilometers per second we can easily calculate the simple speed of light delay over 12,000 kms is 40 msecs. That's for light in a vacuum—in a fiber the speed is reduced by a factor proportional to the index of refraction of the fiber at the wavelength of light used. For typical fibers that's about 2/3, so the speed-of-light delay in a fiber, one way, from Palo Alto to Sydney is about 60 msecs.

_____

[2] According to Steve Mitchell's Great Circle Calculator at
`http://www.atinet.org/~steve/cs150`

Table 10-1.   Data in Flight to Australia.

Link Type	Link Speed (Mbit/sec)	kbyte in Flight
T1	1.5	11
Ethernet	10	75
DS-3	45	338
OC-3	155	1,162

Now let's imagine that this link is being driven by an old crusty 1200-baud modem with a fiber interface. (I know, never mind...it's a thought experiment, OK?) We can send 1200 bits down the fiber in 1 sec, and when we start sending, it takes the first bit 60 msecs to get to its destination.

Now imagine that we've upgraded our modems to something a little more modern and are sending at 155 Mbit/sec. We can send one hundred and fifty-five million bits in the same second, but it *still takes the first bit 60 msecs to get there.*

Why does this matter? Imagine something a little more realistic, say, a T1 line connecting our transpacific computers. If we start sending in Palo Alto at 1.5 Mbits/sec, then 60 msecs later, when the first bit arrives in Sydney, we have transmitted 90,000 bits or a little over 11 kbytes. So, if for some reason, the receiver in Sydney can't accept data right now, it has to send back a message asking us to stop, which will take another 60 msecs to arrive. This means that if we don't want to drop any bits into the Marianas Trench, we need to buffer 90,000 bits twice or about 22 kbytes of data. This is not too bad; round up to a power of two and at today's memory prices spending 32 kbytes of buffering on an active connection doesn't seem too unreasonable.

Let's check out ATM at OC-3 speeds, though. At 155 Mbits/sec, when the first bit arrives in Sydney, 9.3 million bits have been sent—not quite 1.2 Mbytes. That's 2.4 Mbytes to buffer per connection. Even at today's memory prices that's starting to be excessive.

Now let's look back at TCP's sliding-window protocol and think: How big is a window? That is, how much data can the sender send before it must stop and wait for the receiver to ACK it? Well, the usual default is 8 kbytes, which works fine on Ethernets where the nearest neighbor is only a few tens of microseconds away, but on our imaginary California-to-Australia link, it's *terrible*.

If we send 8 kbytes, then wait for an ACK, and then send 8 more, how much are we wasting? Well, we're going to transmit the maximum window size, and then wait for the ACK, which will take 120 msecs. But the computer can send the 8 kbytes in only 423 μsecs, leaving it 119 and a half msec to twiddle its metaphorical thumbs until the ACK gets back from down under. Our throughput will be about 68,300 bytes/sec. On an OC-3 link!

OK, let's crank the window up to the biggest value it can have. To heck with the memory it will take, we need performance! How high can the window size go? Well, according to RFC793, the TCP Standard, there are 16 bits for window size in the TCP header, so a window can be at most 65,536 bytes. How does that do?

Well, we still need to send the 64 kbytes, and then wait for the ACK to come back 120 msecs later. The transmission takes 3.4 msecs, and we wait for the ACK, and our throughput is a bit better than 0.5 Mbyte/sec.

Now this is starting to look respectable. It's 43 percent of an Ethernet. But wait—we're not using an Ethernet, we're using an expensive OC-3. The darn TCP windows just *cannot* be made large enough to get a decent performance!

"But I'm not talking to Australia, I'm just sending data to my company's home office in the next state," you say. Well, the problem persists, but to a lesser degree, depending on distance. Let's work the figures the other way around to see how far one can go with 64 kbyte windows.

What we want is for an ACK to come back by the time we've finished sending 64 kbytes and filling the window, so that the window will open back up and we can keep sending; 64 kbytes is 524,288 bits, and that takes 3.4 msecs to send. We want our ACK back by then, so the time to reach the destination can be at most half that, or 1.7 ms, to allow the data time to get there and for the ACK to come back. (I'm neglecting protocol overhead and the fact that it will take a finite time for enough data to flow in and trigger the ACK.) The propagation speed of light in typical fibers is about 2/3 that of light in vacuum, so in 1.7 ms the light can travel 507 kms or a little over 300 miles.

This is not great; it will work OK in local areas, say a building or campus, and even in a metropolitan area like Sydney or the San Francisco Bay Area. If we go much farther, like, say, from San Francisco to Los Angeles, we start to waste performance waiting for ACKs.

The solution to this problem is big TCP windows, described in Section 10.3.

10.2.4 Slowstart Considered Harmful

"Slowstart" is the term for the technique of slowly opening the window at the beginning of a TCP congestion so as to avoid overwhelming intermediate routers with bursts of packets.

In the "traditional" configuration (Figure 10-1), we have a workstation attached to an Ethernet, that accesses the Internet through a router attached to both this Ethernet and to a 56 kbit[3] serial link to a peer router, where there's another Ethernet and a server.

Now the host wishes to make a TCP connection to the server. It does the three-way handshake and is ready to send data. So what does it do? It immedi-

---

[3] Imagine this was in ancient times, at least four years ago.

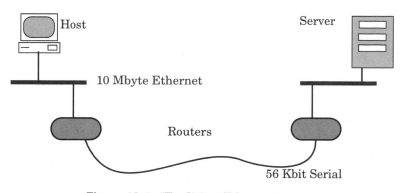

Figure 10-1. "Traditional" Internet setup.

ately sends 8 kbytes of data—a window's worth. That's six packets, given the Ethernet packet size of about 1500 bytes.

These packets all arrive at the router at 10 Mbit/sec, but they can only leave the router at 56 kbit. Not a problem, you say, the sending host will just wait until an ACK comes back from the server to okay sending more.

Ah, but let's imagine that the poor router is heavily loaded with traffic. An Ethernet can deliver data to the router much faster than it can send it out, and it has finite-sized buffers. If there is a persistently high load, some of these six packets may well get dropped.

In this case, the sender will wait for ACKS, not get them, and retransmit the packets. Wham! They get dropped again. Sure, one or two may get through, but the net is now in "congestion collapse"; the link is saturated but no real traffic is getting through.

The solution invented by Van Jacobsen of the Lawrence Berkeley Lab was the slowstart algorithm [Jacobson 1988]: at the beginning of a TCP connection, send one data packet and wait for the ACK, then send two and wait, and so on, gradually opening the window to the optimum size.

This avoids having the sender hammer on the routers with large amounts of data before finding out if there's enough free bandwidth to accept the traffic.

So what does this have to do with ATM? With an ATM backbone the situation is exactly reversed (Figure 10-2): Instead of a slow skinny pipe in the middle of the net there's a big fat fast one that can take everything an Ethernet can throw at it and then some. Now, especially if we have a long link in the middle, by the time slowstart has the window fully open we probably could have transmitted our whole file and been done!

Clearly in a modern TCP/IP we need some selective implementations of the classic algorithms that can adapt to the actual link characteristics.

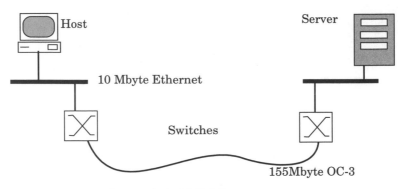

Figure 10-2. "ATM" Internet setup.

10.2.5 Deadlock

When using default TCP parameters there is a possibility of severe degradation of throughput over very high-speed links, as was shown in [Moldeklev 1994]. Moldeklev and his colleagues were measuring the throughput of some early ATM cards with various combinations of TCP socket buffer sizes, and observed that while they usually got throughput of around 20 Mbit/sec, for some settings the throughput mysteriously dropped to a mere 0.65–0.16 Mbit—not even as good as Ethernet!

What was happening was that with large packets and certain size receive buffers, the sender could not send enough data to trigger a window update from the receiver, and there was not enough space in the sender's buffer to form another MSS-sized segment. The TCP "Nagle" algorithm was preventing the transmission of segments smaller than the maximum segment size (MSS) if there are outstanding unacknowledged bytes so as to avoid large numbers of tiny packets in interactive use, and the receiver wasn't acknowledging because its buffer wasn't full enough.

The only reason any data got through was that the receiver's 200 ms TCP timer would go off and force acknowledgment of the received data anyway, breaking the deadlock and allowing another one or two packets to be transmitted.

The simplest solution was to turn off the Nagle algorithm (some TCP stacks now have an option to allow this to be done by the administrator), rather than by changing the TCP code.

10.2.6 Sequence Number Wrapping

These are not the only bad things that can happen to TCP when link speeds get fast. The reliability of TCP relies on the sequence number and a bound on the lifetime of a segment. As long as the bit sequence number doesn't wrap until all of the segments that might conflict have either been delivered or timed out, all is OK.

Consider Table 10-2 (taken with slight modification from RFC 1323). Here we can see, for various link speeds, how long it will take to transmit 2^{32} bytes, which is another way of saying how long will it be before we have to reuse old sequence numbers. RFC 793 defines the maximum segment lifetime (MSL) to be 2 mins, or 120 secs, so at FDDI speeds and above we're uncomfortably close to (or well into!) the danger zone. All it takes is a packet to get stuck in a router somewhere for a few hundred milliseconds and then come out and be delivered.

Table 10-2. Time for Sequence Number Wrapping.

Network	bits/sec	bytes/sec	Time to Wrap
ARPANET	56 k	7 k	3.6 d
T1/DS1	1.5 M	190 k	3 h
Ethernet	10 M	1.25 M	30 min
DS3	45 M	5.6 M	380 sec
FDDI/Fast Ethernet	100 M	12.5 M	170 sec
OC-3	155 M	19.4 M	109 sec

But wait! It gets worse!

Despite the discussion in RFC793 about clocks for MSL timeouts, it is almost universal practice in the Internet to use the time-to-live field instead and decrement it once per hop. TCP segments can live much longer than 2 mins.

But wait! It gets better! Luckily this problem only surfaces when a TCP stream transmits more than 2^{32} bytes, or 4.3 gigabytes. While long-lived connections can generate this much traffic,[4] it's rare (so far) for this to take place at full link speed, and when it does it's usually within a well-controlled network. Further, a lot of streaming protocols like video and audio that can generate a lot of data over a connection tend not to use TCP at all.

Still, what can be done to prevent this? The Protection Against Sequence Number Wrapping (PAWS) algorithm uses time stamps on TCP segments to guard against accepting old delayed segments as valid new ones. To simplify a bit, it keeps the time stamp of the most recent in-sequence segment processed for this TCP connection and rejects segments with time stamps older than this.

---

[4] Have you checked how many bytes come in every day on a full NNTP Usenet feed lately?

10.3 Big Windows

RFC1323 is titled *TCP Extensions for High Performance* and gives a specification for one way to deal with the tiny-window problem, the TCP Window Scale Option (Figure 10-3).

Figure 10-3. TCP Window Scale Option.

This redefines the window value to be 32 bits instead of the usual 16. The value is still carried in the 16-bit window field of the TCP header, so during connection establishment the two hosts negotiate a *scale factor* that will be applied to this value. A 3-byte option is set in the initial SYN packet.

If the other host also includes a Window Scale Option in its SYN packet, then window scaling will be used. If a host implements this option but for whatever reason doesn't wish to scale its own windows it can send a shift of 0.

When a system wishes to send a window size, it will right-shift the value by the number of bits it sent in its Window Scale Option, and the receiving system will recover the value by left-shifting it that amount.

This means that the window values will be rounded off some, but that was deemed acceptable, since tiny adjustments in a large window don't cause much of a problem, and more importantly, the TCP header need not be changed.

So, for example, if host A sent a shift factor of 8 to host B (Table 10-3), then instead of the old window range of 0 to $65535(2^{16}-1)$, it can send from 0 to $16,776,960$ ($2^{24}-255$). The table summarizes the window ranges for some sample shift values. Note that 0 is always 0 no matter how far you shift it, and that shift values of more than 16 are not practical, since the maximum value begins to be larger than 32 bits.

Table 10-3. Window Scale Option.

Shift Value	Upper Limit	Step Size
0	65,535	1
1	131,070	2
2	262,140	4
4	1,048,560	16
8	16,776,960	256
16	4,294,901,760	65,536

Using the maximum possible window shift factor of 16, the window can be nearly 4 gigabytes! How far would this let us run our link?

Well, it's 3.4×10^{10} bits, which takes 221.7 secs to send at OC3 rates. In that time, light can travel forty-four million kms in a fiber or sixty-six million kms in vacuum. That's to the Moon and back 83 times! I think that this will let TCP operate at its best potential until the Internet is extended well beyond the Moon.

10.4 Machine and OS Architecture for High Performance

One of the big bottlenecks in network performance is copying the data and check-summing it. Many protocol implementations make at least two copies: first the data are copied from a buffer on the network card into a buffer in the operating system, and then the data are copied into the user-program's buffer. Eliminating the copying by moving the data directly from the network card to the user-program's buffer will allow the computer to do less work moving the same amount of data. Either the data will move faster, since there's less to do to move it, or the computer will be able to do more work while moving data, or both.

10.4.1 The Afterburner

Based on some ideas in [Jacobson 90], Hewlett-Packard implemented an experimental Fiber-Distributed Data Interface (FDDI) interface called After-burner. This interface plugged into the graphics bus of a Hewlett-Packard work-station so that a high-bandwidth path to the processor was available. It could just as well have used the normal memory bus, but graphics memory was not required to support error correction.

The card had triple-ported video memory, with two ports used to connect transmit and receive controllers, and the third connected to the physical medium transmit-and-receive hardware.

Experiments with this interface, comparing a "standard" Berkeley socket implementation with one that used the video ram as a source of kernel network buffers, showed that the throughput was approximately doubled by eliminating copy from kernel memory to the network card. It was easily able to saturate a 100 Mbit FDDI link, which was no mean feat with those ancient, slow 1990 vintage CPUs.

10.4.2 Protocol Engine

The Protocol Engine was an effort by the ill-fated start-up company Proto-col Engines to build a VLSI chip to help with networking. It contained a special-ized RISC processor and a "protocol parser" that could identify the protocol that a packet belonged to and arrange for it to be CRC'd and checksummed before the host processor ever saw it. By moving the per-byte overhead of checksumming from the host processor to the network card, a great savings in effort was achieved.

Alas, schedule slippage and nervous investors doomed the company before they could ship any products, but their ideas influenced modern network interface design.

10.4.3 Protocol Stack Improvements

Recently there has been some work done on implementing so-called "zero-copy" protocol stacks, where the data is copied directly from the network to the user's buffer, eliminating all copying of data by TCP and the operating system.

[Kay 1993a] and [Kay 1993b] describe actual measurements of data-copying overhead in a typical Unix workstation. Not surprisingly, checksumming and other data-touching operations dominate the time spent. This was expected, of course, but verifiable measurements showing it to be true are useful.

The authors present some possible ways to deal with this, from checksum assist in hardware to selectively disabling IP checksums when end-to-end transmission is protected, as it is on an Ethernet with its CRCs. (Of course, once a packet enters a router, the checksum becomes essential; the Ethernet CRC will protect a packet corrupted by a failing router just as carefully as it does an intact one.)

Improving the checksum code to take advantage of processor pipelining and cache effects is shown to be useful; in essence, since cache misses while copying the data leave the processor idle for a few instructions, why not calculate the checksum while waiting for the next data?

[Chu 1996] describes a zero-copy feature for Sun Microsystem's Solaris operating system. With checksumming hardware in the networking card and clever use of virtual memory remapping, TCP never has to touch the data at all, just process the headers. The Usenix paper cited also describes other zero-copy architectures.

[Thadani 1995] describes additional work at Sun Labs, using fast buffers (fbufs), which allows applications to explicitly pass and receive buffers to and from the kernel TCP module, eliminating the need for a copy at the kernel-user interface.

10.5 Summary

In summary, you can't just buy an ATM card, slam it into your PC and expect to get 155 Mbits end-to-end. All of the parts of the network, from the application down to the wire, have to be carefully considered.

The best way to solve the problem is to measure your network performance, decide why it's not what you want, fix it, and iterate until it's fast enough. Some of the things to check are:

- **Big MTU**—Big packets incur less per-packet overhead for the whole transfer.
- **Big windows**—Necessary to keep the "long fat pipe" full. Use the RFC1323 Window Scale Option if you can.
- **Big socket buffers**.
- **Good machine architecture**—An ISA-bus PC just can't keep up, and even some more powerful machines have components that were fine when an Ethernet was fast, but aren't up to snuff today.
- **Careful design** of applications to make sure they can handle the data stream.

It can be done! Good luck.

Looking Toward the Future—
Research Directions

In this chapter we'll examine some of the directions that research and development are going in the ATM field. This is by no means a complete list, just some of the more interesting areas under study. I'll give information on how to find out more about each topic.

I'm deliberately not running down a list of ATM equipment manufacturers since there are plenty of information sources for that, and there are new products every day.

Please understand that my failure to include a project here should not be construed to mean that it isn't interesting. There simply isn't room to run down every ATM project underway. The list of projects changed constantly too; I'm trying to mention projects that are long-lived, have interesting results, or both.

11.1 Practical WAN Experience: Real-Life Testbeds

Quite a few so-called "Gigabit Testbeds" have been built over the last few years in order to deploy and test high-speed networking hardware and software. Quite a few, but not all, have used ATM as their network technology.

Some of these testbeds use OC-3 links, which at 155 Mbits are hardly giga-bit speeds. Some wags call this a "Government Gigabit," it being what is left after taxes.

11.1.1 BLANCA

BLANCA is a testbed supported by the National Science Foundation. It connects AT&T Bell Laboratories in New Jersey, The National Center for Supercomputing Applications in Illinois, The University of Wisconsin at Madison, University of California Berkeley, Lawrence Berkeley National Laboratory, Lawrence Livermore National Laboratory, and Sandia Labs, all in California.

The backbone network was provided by AT&T Bell Laboratories through the XUNET Communications Research Program.

For more information:

```
http://www.ncsa.uiuc.edu/General/CC/CCBLANCA.html
http://www.ncsa.uiuc.edu/General/CC/CCXunet.html
```

11.1.2 Canarie's NTN

CANARIE is the Canadian Network for the Advancement of Research, Industry and Education, a Canadian nonprofit organization dedicated to the development of the communications infrastructure in Canada. The National Test Network (NTN) is a large[1] TCP/IP network spanning Canada from St. Johns to Vancouver, made up of DS-3 and OC-3 links. Researchers and developers are encouraged to use the network to work on high-speed applications, such as multimedia distance learning, medical imaging, and teleconferencing. Support for "native" ATM as well as TCP/IP is available.

For more information:

```
http://www.canarie.ca/eng/ntn/main.html
```

11.1.3 MAGIC-II

MAGIC-II is a follow-on project building on the work of the now-complete MAGIC-I. It is sponsored by the Corporation for National Research Initiatives (CNRI). CNRI is a nonprofit organization that sponsors research to benefit "the public interest," mainly network information technologies.

MAGIC-I built a wide-area TCP/IP network based on ATM OC-48 links that interconnected research sites in California, Kansas, Minnesota, and South Dakota. MAGIC-II builds on this work and extends it to provide real-time terrain visualization and distributed storage. Applications to use these facilities include military operations, including battle simulations; intelligence analysis and simulation of natural disasters.

---

[1] CANARIE claims it is the world's largest high-speed test network.

To achieve these goals, several hard problems need to be solved. The participants must manage multiple disparate terabyte datasets, access and process them in real-time and deliver the data over high-speed datalinks to a wide variety of host computers.

For more information:
http://www.magic.net/

11.1.4 BAGNet

The Bay Area Gigabit Network was made up of 15 research and educational sites in the San Francisco Bay area, interconnected with OC-3 ATM links provided by Pacific Bell and funded by CalREN, the California Research and Educational Network, a nonprofit corporation. The motivation was to provide a "teleseminar" capability. Many of the participating organizations sponsor seminars, talks, and presentations that are interesting, but driving through the notably bad Bay Area traffic for two hours each way to hear a 45-minute talk is understandably unpopular.

If the presentations could be broadcast in high quality using ATM technologygym, perhaps more people could "attend" the talks.

BAGNet used Classical IP over ATM with PVCs, since the backbone switches did not support signaling when BAGNet was being set up. Due to limitations in the backbone switches, a maximum of four hosts per site was allowed. A fully connected point-to-point PVC mesh was established, and four point-to-multipoint PVCs per site enabled a form of multicast to work.

Regular Mbone tools (vic, vat, sd) were used and worked well in the high-speed environment. After a shakedown period several sites transmitted regular seminars until the CalREN grant expired in 1996.

For more information:
http://george.lbl.gov/bagnet.html

11.1.5 SPARTAN

SPARTAN is the "SPrint Applied Research parTners Advanced Network," a research network with backbone links supplied by Sprint Corporation. Participants include Sprint's Advanced Technology Laboratory (ATL) in California, Digital Equipment Corporation's Systems Research Center, Xerox' Palo Alto Research Center, SRI International, the University of Kansas, and Sprint's Technology Integration and Operations Center (TIOC) in Kansas.

Sites in California connect to the Sprint ATL via OC-3 links. The ATL connects to the TIOC over a DS-3 that's actually a protection circuit. The TIOC connects to the University of Kansas with an OC-3 and also provides connectivity to the MAGIC-II testbed.

For more information:
http://www.spartan.net/spartan/

11.1.6 Next Generation Internet

The Next Generation Internet (NGI) is a U.S. Government-sponsored research initiative to provide high-performance networking to the U.S. Research community and U.S. Government agencies.

Characteristics of the fully deployed NGI will include:

- Real-time multimedia capabilities with guaranteed QoS
- Ability to manipulate extremely large amounts of data
- Secure remote access to supercomputers and the ability to "cluster" multiple supercomputers to provide advanced capabilities
- Shared virtual environments providing remote collaboration to researchers.

For more information:
http://www.ngi.gov/

11.2 Interesting Academic Research

11.2.1 Secure Signaling

Current ATM Signaling standards provide no mechanism for authentication of the information passed along with the signaling messages. Many researchers feel that it is essential to provide this so that connections can be accepted or rejected based on the knowledge that, for instance, the calling party really is who he says he is and isn't an imposter.

Some work on secure signaling and its application to firewalls was done at Xerox PARC (also sponsored by Purdue and Sprint Labs) and can be found in [Schuba 97].

11.2.2 The Cambridge DAN

The Computer Laboratory Systems Research Group at Cambridge University, U.K., has been conducting interesting research in using ATM.

Past work includes the Fairisle experimental ATM Switch and the Desk Area Network (DAN). The DAN multimedia workstation was built around the Fairisle switches as the main bus. All communications between peripherals such as disks, audio and video inputs and outputs, and even between the processor and main memory are carried by ATM cells.

Currently they are working on the "Home Area Network," using ATM25 to build a network with ATM service to the home, supporting high-quality audiovisual services as well as traditional networking. Control of cheap, stupid (but fast!) ATM devices by proxies is an aspect of this work that should produce useful results.

For more information:

`http://www.cl.cam.ac.uk/Research/SRG/netos.html`

11.2.3 Comet

The COMET Group of the Center for Telecommunications Research at Columbia University, New York, conducts research in software for networks. They focus on

- Open Signaling for ATM
- Real-Time Transport Protocol
- Session Initiation Protocol
- Wireless ATM.

For more information:

`http://startide.ctr.columbia.edu/comet/Intro.html`

11.2.4 SwitchWare

SwitchWare is a project of the University of Pennsylvania and Bellcore, wherein the deployment of new network services is enabled by allowing the input and output ports of a switching element to be programmable. The programs are carried in messages to the port, which interprets the programs and performs the appropriate actions.

The developers are being careful to balance generality and extensibility against security and administrative resource allocation. The benefits would be

- being able to keep up with the "technology curve" by reprogramming instead of standardizing and buying new equipment
- allowing user-specified extensibility
- making formal verification methods applicable.

For more information:

`http://www.cis.upenn.edu/~jms/SoftSwitch.html`

11.3 Interesting Developments in the Industry

New product announcements for ATM and ATM-related software and hardware seem to come out in every new issue of the trade publications. Rather than run down who has a new switch with what cool feature—information sure to be obsolete before you read this—I'll look at a few truly interesting technologies.

11.3.1 IP Switching

This technology, invented by Ipsilon Networks, Inc., combines ATM switching with an IP router. The entire ATM protocol stack has been discarded, eliminating signaling, address resolution, and all the rest of the complicated ball of wax that is ATM.

The switch runs, instead, a standard IP routing protocol and Ipsilon's General Switch Management Protocol [RFC1987]. Upon initialization, the switch software establishes virtual circuits to the neighboring switches and forwards IP datagrams over them.

So far it's just a fancy router built on an ATM switch; the processor doing the forwarding is a bottleneck. To alleviate this, the switch notices the characteristics of the packets as it's forwarding them and makes a decision about whether a flow of packets, say, between two hosts, is a candidate for being switched directly. If so, it creates a circuit through its fabric for it. Then it sends a message to the downstream neighbor—the source of the packets—telling it the new VPC/VCI to send on, and to the upstream node, telling it that packets to a certain destination will be coming on a certain VPI/VCI. (The IP Flow Management Protocol [RFC1953] describes these messages.)

Point-to-point and multicast flows are supported and QoS conditions can be enforced. Ipsilon is making the technology available to the research community and has announced products using IP Switching.

For more information:

```
http://www.ipsilon.com/technology/
```

11.3.2 Tag Switching

Tag switching is a scheme from Cisco to combine high-performance layer 2 (datalink) switching with the scalability and functionality of layer 3 (network) routing. The basic idea is to give packets tags at the edge of a network using this technology. The packets can then be easily switched through the network with little processing needed.

In fact, it's very similar to the way that ATM cells are routed through an ATM network. Think of the tag as an ATM cell header, with the virtual-circuit identifier being changed at each hop as the cell (or packet) travels through the net.

The difference is that the packets need not be shredded into cells and reassembled at each router when the Cisco tag is applied.

The Tag Distribution Protocol allows switches and routers to exchange information about tags that are active in the network.

Cisco has published some Internet Drafts describing the technology, and stated that it will license patents for no or nominal fees if IETF standards require their technology.

For more information:

```
http://www.cisco.com/warp/public/732/tag/index.html
```

How to Find
Standards Documents

$\mathbf{H}$ere is information on how to get standards documents relevant to IP, ATM, and the Internet. This information is believed to be correct at the time this book was written, but cannot be guaranteed.

A good starting point for further research is the Cell Relay Retreat, a WWW site maintained at the University of Indiana:

```
http://cell-relay.indiana.edu/
```

IETF

For general information about the IETF, the best place to go is the IETF homepage at

```
http://www.ietf.org
```

You'll find background information on the IETF, schedules of upcoming meetings, online proceedings of some past meetings, and pointers to RFCs and Internet Drafts.

There are several ways to get IETF documents. There are numerous World Wide Web collections, including one run by the Internic

```
http://www.internic.net/ds/dspg0intdoc.html
```

and the site maintained by the RFC Editor, John Postel

```
http://www.isi.edu/rfc-editor/
```

These Web sites have RFCs, Internet Drafts, FYIs and more.
In addition to WWW access, you can get them by FTP and e-mail.
For FTP, try one of these sites:

```
ftp://DS.INTERNIC.NET/rfc
ftp://NIS.NSF.NET/internet/documents/rfc
ftp://FTP.ISI.EDU/in-notes/
ftp://SRC.DOC.IC.AC.UK/rfc
```

For e-mail, one of the following should work:

- Send a message to

  ```
  mailserv@ds.internic.net
  ```

  with

  ```
  document-by-name rfcNNN
  ```

  as the body.

- Send a message to

  ```
  NIS-INFO@NIS.NSF.NET
  ```

  with no subject and

  ```
  send rfcNNN.txt
  ```

  as the body.

A WWW search with any search engine for "How to get RFCs" should turn up even more possibilities.

Individual Working Groups often have their own web sites as well; the one most relevant to this book is the Internetworking over NBMA (ION) group whose charter can be found at

```
http://www.ietf.org/html.charters/ion-charter.html
```

ITU

The Web site for the ITU is at

```
http://www.itu.ch/
```

You can find a list of ITU Recommendations at

```
http://www.itu.ch/publications/itu-t/itutrec.htm
```

Some, but not all documents have abstracts available, and all can be purchased, either at the "On-line bookstore" or by subscribing to the Telecom Information Exchange Services (TIES).

The practice of charging significant amounts of money for standards documents is a controversial one, especially to the traditionally open organizations like the IETF. On the one hand, the ITU needs income to operate, and selling documents is a reasonable way to make some cash.[1] On the other hand, some people believe the key to wide acceptance and implementation of standards is to distribute them free of charge to anyone who's interested. Whatever side of the debate you are on, it comes down to the fact that the ITU charges for documents and the IETF doesn't, and it would be an uphill struggle to get either to change.

A few key ATM documents are available on other servers; a WWW search engine such as AltaVista or HotBot should turn them up.

ATM Forum

The main ATM Forum Web site is at

```
http://www.atmforum.com/
```

Approved ATM Forum technical specifications (that have passed through the ATM Forum process and voted on) are available at

```
http://www.atmforum.com/atmforum/specs/specs.html
```

Paper copies are available for reasonable fees. For ordering information visit the web page or contact:

The ATM Forum Worldwide Headquarters
Attn: Tammy Hess
FAX: +1-415-949-6705

The ATM Forum Europe Office
Attn: Leen Hofmans
FAX: +32.2.732.8485

The ATM Forum Asia-Pacific Office
Attn: Sayuri Takazawa
FAX: +81.3.3438.3698

The UNI signaling specification is also published by Prentice Hall, Englewood Cliffs, NJ, and the Ancorage Accord by McGraw-Hill, New York.

---

[1] A sentiment I'm sure my publisher will agree with.

If you want access to documents representing works-in-progress, about the only way is to either become a member of the ATM Forum or, if your organization is already a member, discover who in your organization is the representative and ask them for access. "The General Public" is not usually allowed access to unfinished documents and contributions.

Well-Known VCCs

Well-Known VCCs.

VPI	VCI	Definition
0	1	Meta-signaling
0	2	General Broadcast Signaling
0	3	F4 OAM Flows within a VPC segment
0	4	F4 OAM flows end-to-end
0	5	Q.2931/UNI signaling messages
0	6	Resource Management (RM)
0	16	ILMI Default VCC
0	17	LANE Default Configuration-DIRECT VCC

ATM Software

There are a few freely available ATM and networking software packages available on the Internet. Most of them can be used for private, research, or evaluation purposes without fees. Of course, if you plan to use them be sure to check out the copyright notices, disclaimers, or license terms first; and if you're going to build a product on one of these packages, be sure to have your lawyers talk to their lawyers first.

VINCE

VINCE is the "Vendor Independent Network Control Entity," a freely available implementation of ATM signaling that implements UNI 3.0, and Fore Systems' proprietary SPANS protocol. Drivers for a few common ATM cards and switches are provided.

VINCE was developed by the Research Networks section of the Center for Computational Science at the Naval Research Laboratory, with support from the Advanced Research Projects Agency (ARPA) and NAVSEA. See

```
http://www.nrl.navy.mil/CCS/atm/vince.html
```

VINCE is currently not being maintained, having been replaced by SEAN.

173

SEAN

SEAN, the Signaling Entity for ATM Networks, is the successor to VINCE. SEAN was also developed at the Naval Research Lab and provides

- a UNI-3.1 host ATM signaling stack,

with

- a C++ Native ATM application programming interface, and
- support for RFC1577-style IP over ATM.

  SEAN can be downloaded from

  ```
  http://www.nrl.navy.mil/CCS/sean/
  ```

HARP

The Advanced Networking Group at Network Computing Services, Inc. have implemented the Host ATM Research Platform, called HARP. The latest version supports the IETF Classical IP scheme for a variety of ATM interfaces on FreeBSD and SunOS 4. It can be downloaded from

```
http://www.msci.magic.net/
```

and is free for noncommercial purposes.

UNI 3.1 in Java

A demonstration of UNI3.1 signaling in a Java Applet is at

```
http://www.ultranet.com/~dhudek/junidemo1.shtml
```

If you're confused about how signaling works, visit this page with a Java-capable browser and watch the messages flow back and forth. There are point-to-point and point-to-multipoint examples. All will become clear!

x-ATM Toolkit from UIUC

The University of Illinois at Urbana-Champaign released a toolkit for building ATM protocols on the x-Kernel operating system

```
http://choices.cs.uiuc.edu/x-ATM/x-ATM.htmlstem
```

ATM Software for Linux, FreeBSD, NetBSD...

ATM drivers for FreeBSD are available at

```
ftp://dworkin.wustl.edu/dist/bsd/
```

and have been incorporated into the latest releases.

An experimental ATM for Linux distribution is available at

```
http://lrcwww.epfl.ch/linux-atm/
```

through the courtesy of the Laboratoire de Réseaux de Communication in Switzerland.

Another Linux-ATM kit is the KU ATM Tool Chest, available from the University of Kansas at

```
http://www.tisl.ukans.edu/Projects/Linux_ATM/
eni-atm.html
```

ATM Simulators

The Berkeley Ptolemy simulator

```
http://ptolemy.eecs.berkeley.edu/)
```

is useful in all sorts of simulation and research.

The National Institute of Standards and Technology (NIST) ATM simulator is described at

```
http://isdn.ncsl.nist.gov/misc/hsnt/prj_atm-sim.html
```

It is useful as a network planning or protocol analysis tool, offering interactive modeling and performance analysis.

LAN Emulation Starter Kit

Digital Equipment Corporation (DEC) has made a starter kit of software for LAN Emulation available at

```
http://www.networks.digital.com:80/dr/atmkit/
index.html
```

This package is designed to work with the Trillium signaling code. Token Ring, ILMI LECS location, LANE over PVCs, and QoS are not supported.

Commercial Signaling Packages

Several companies offer commercial, supported signaling packages. This is by no means an exhaustive list. Inclusion or exclusion of a particular company or product should not be taken as an endorsement or condemnation.

- Inverness Systems:

  ```
  http://www.inverness.co.il/html/index.html
  ```

- Cellware Broadband

  ```
  http://www.cellware.de/
  ```

- Harris and Jeffries

  ```
  http://www.hjinc.com/product.html
  ```

- Telogy Networks

  ```
  http://www.telogy.com/
  ```

- Trillium Digital Systems, Inc.

  ```
  http://www.trillium.com/
  ```

- Bellcore

  ```
  http://www.bellcore.com/
  ```

Glossary

ATM Glossaries

The ATM Forum has a nice WWW glossary located at
`http://www.atmforum.com/atmforum/library/glossary/glosspage.html`[1]
Another glossary is contained in ITU Recommendation I.113, "Living List."
The Cell-Relay Retreat has pointers to several ATM dictionaries at
`http://cell-relay.indiana.edu/cell-relay/`
`ReferenceSources.html`

A Real Glossary

In case you don't have a web browser handy here's a glossary you can refer to while reading the book.

---

[1] While working on this book I checked this URL and found it had changed; if it changes again before you read this you can probably find it from the ATM Forum Home page: `http://www.atmforum.com/`

10baseT—Ethernet carried over unshielded twisted-pair cables. The "10" refers to the Ethernet signaling speed of 10 Mbits/sec; "base" to the fact that Ethernet is a baseband technology, and "T" means "twisted."

AAL—ATM Adaptation Layer. A scheme for encoding packets into one of more ATM cells.

AAL1—An AAL designed for Constant Bit Rate traffic.

AAL2—An AAL used for Variable Bit Rate traffic.

AAL3/4—An AAL used for data.

AAL5—An AAL used for data, designed to be simpler than AAL3/4.

ABR—Available Bit Rate. A traffic class defined by the ATM Forum for data traffic insensitive to delays and without strict bandwidth requirements.

ACK—A TCP Acknowledgment.

Acknowledgment—A TCP message that confirms receipt of data up to a certain point in the stream.

address—A code for identifying a communications end point. There are several types of addresses discussed in this book: ATM, Ethernet or MAC, and IP.

Admission—Sometimes "Call Admission." The practice of deciding whether to accept a connection based on the traffic parameters requested and the current state of the network.

AFI—Authority and Format Identifier. The part of an ATM address that indicates how to decode the remainder.

AIS—Alarm Indication Signal. A SONET message indicating an error condition.

AOL—America On-Line. A large on-line service.

ARP—Address Resolution Protocol. Given an IP address, one finds its MAC address using ARP so that packets can be addressed to it.

ARPA—Advanced Research Projects Authority. A branch of the U.S. Department of Defense that funds research in, among other areas, computer networking.

ASN.1—Abstract Syntax Notation version 1. Language used for describing SNMP Management Information Bases, among others.

ATM—Asynchronous Transfer Mode. What this book is about.

BADLAN—Experimental ATM project at Xerox PARC.

bandwidth reservations—Reserving a portion of a network's available bandwidth for a connection.

baseband—Digital data transmission with one signal or channel per "wire." For instance, a typical modem will transmit one signal over a single phone line. Contrast *broadband*, q.v.

BayLISA—Bay Area Large Installation System Administrators, a professional organization of system administrators in the San Francisco Bay Area that uses the Mbone to transmit their meetings.

BBN—Bolt, Beranak, and Newman. Consulting firm active in the design and implementation of the Internet. Spun off an ISP, BBNPlaNet.

BCD—Binary Coded Decimal, a method of representing numbers in computer memory.

BER—Bit Error Rate.

B-ISDN—Broadband Integrated Services Digital Network. The ITU's grand vision for the future of public networks, which ATM is supposed to make possible.

bit—The smallest unit of information; a 1 or a 0.

bridge—A type of network equipment that joins two or more physical segments of network into a single logical network as viewed from the network layer.

broadband—Digital data transmission with more than one signal or channel per "wire." For instance, a SONET OC-3 multiplexes several T-1 signals over a single optical fiber.

Broadcast—To send a packet to all hosts on a given network or portion of a network.

BUS—Broadcast and Unknown Server; the LAN Emulation entity that implements broadcast and multicast.

byte—Usually 8 bits in modern machines; the smallest unit of storage allocation.

call reference—An identifier used by ATM signaling algorithms to identify connection requests.

CBR—Constant Bit Rate, a traffic class used for data with constant bandwidth needs and high sensitivity to packet delay.

CCITT—Comittée Consultatif Internationale de Téléphonie and Télégraphie; the predecessor of the International Telecommunications Union.

CDVT—Cell Delay Variation.

cell—The 53-byte packet used by ATM protocols.

checksum—A number formed by summing the bytes of a packet or portion of a packet; used for error detection.

Class A address—A large block of IP addresses, characterized by an 8-bit network part and a 24-bit host part.

Class B address—A medium-sized block of IP addresses, characterized by a 16-bit network part and a 16-bit host part.

Class C address—A small block of IP addresses, characterized by a 24-bit network part and an 8-bit host part.

client—A computer or program that requests services from a server.

ClusterControlVC—The virtual circuit used by a MARS (q.v.) for control traffic.

Configuration Direct VCC—A bidirectional VCC set up by a LANE Client to its LECS (configuration server) so that it can figure out how to connect to its ELAN.

Control Direct VCC—A bidirectional VCC set up between the LEC and the LES so that the LEC can "register" with the LES.

Control Distribute VCC—A unidirectional multipoint VCC from the LES back to the clients it serves.

CRC—Cyclic Redundancy Check. Scheme for detecting and correcting (some) errors in data transmissions.

CRC32—CRC used in Ethernet and AAL5.

Data Direct VCC—A bidirectional VCC connecting two LANE clients that wish to exchange data.

datagram—A packet that contains enough information to allow it to be delivered to the destination. IP packets are datagrams because they contain the global address of the destination; ATM cells are not because they rely on the internal state of the ATM network to ensure that they arrive.

DCC—Data Country Code; a format for ATM addresses organized by country.

domain—An administrative collection of hosts, typically belonging to a single entity or type of entity. For example, all hosts on the Xerox network belong to the xerox.com domain.

Domain Name Service (DNS)—A service that enables hierarchical administration of the name-to-IP-address mappings.

DSP—Digital Signal Processing. Performing transformations on digitally sampled signals, often with special-purpose hardware.

DVMRP—Distance-Vector Multicast Routing Protocol.

E.164—Number of ITU recommendation for ATM address formats.

ELAN—Emulated LAN.

encapsulation—The technique of wrapping up a packet as the data or payload in another packet, as TCP packets are put into IP packets.

end station—ATM-speak for a computer attached to an ATM network; an ATM entity that is not a switch.

entity—Any machine that participates in ATM protocols.

ESI—End System Identifier.

Ethernet—A LAN technology operating at 10 Mbit/sec using Carrier Sense, Multiple Access with Collision Detection (CSMA/CD). A registered trademark of The Document Company, Xerox.

FDDI—Fiber-Distributed Data Interface. A networking technology running at 100 Mbit/sec, and using fiber-optic rings and token passing.

FIN—The TCP FINish flag; used to signal that one side of a TCP connection is done.

firewall—A computer or router configured to restrict access to a private network.

fragments—Pieces of an IP packet that has been broken up so as to traverse a network with an MTU smaller than the packet size.

frame—A packet from the network layer encapsulated with required headers and trailers for the physical medium.

FTP—File Transfer Protocol. Internet protocol used for transferring bulk data from machine to machine.

global call reference—A special call reference, coded as zero, used to affect all calls on a given channel or switch.

Gopher—An information retrieval protocol, a kind of text-based predecessor to the World Wide Web.

half-closed—The state of a TCP connection when one side has closed the connection (i.e., sent a packet with FIN set) but the other side has not. This is not necessarily a transient state; it can persist for a long time.

HDTV—High Definition TV. The "standard" for advanced digital broadcast television. Actually a set of competing standards being hotly argued about at this writing.

host—A computer attached to a network.

IAB—Internet Advisory Board.

IANA—Internet Assigned Numbers Authority. The body that makes sure that numbers used in the Internet for protocol identity, "well-known" ports and so on, don't conflict.

ICD—International Code Designator. A format of ATM addresses used by International Organizations.

ID—Internet Draft; IETF documents "in progress." May eventually become RFCs.

IDP—Initial Domain Part. A part of an ATM address that identifies the domain it is associated with.

IEEE—The Institute of Electrical and Electronics Engineers, a professional society.

IESG—Internet Engineering Steering Group. Body that oversees the IETF.

IETF—Internet Engineering Task Force. Group that creates, implements, and updates Internet Standards.

IGMP—Internet Group Management Protocol. How membership in multicast groups is managed.

ILMI—Interim Local Management Interface. ATM Forum scheme for remote management of ATM equipment; also used by end nodes to discover information about the network as they initialize.

Information Elements—Data needed in ATM signaling messages, coded as "type-length-value."

Integrated Service—A communications service that provides many types of service with the same connection: voice, data, video, and so on.

internet—A collection of networks connected together to form a larger network.

Internet—With a capital 'I', the global collection of interconnected IP networks.

IP multicast—The technique of transmitting a single packet to multiple interested recipients.

ISDN—Integrated Services Digital Network. Scheme whereby one can receive phone service and data service over the same wires.

ISOC—Internet Society. Sponsors the organizations that oversee the Internet.

ISP—Internet Service Provider. A commercial vendor of Internet connectivity and services.

ITU—International Telecommunications Union.

ITU-T—Telecommunications Standardization Sector of the ITU.

LAN—Local Area Network.

LANE—LAN Emulation; the ATM Forum's scheme to provide ATM service to existing applications by simulating a LAN.

LANE bridges—A device to bridge LAN frames onto a LANE network.

leaf nodes—If you consider a point-to-multipoint virtual circuit as a tree with the sender at the root, then the receivers of the traffic are leaves.

leaf-initiated join—Technique whereby computers wishing to join a point-to-multipoint circuit as leaf nodes may do so without having to communicate with the sender. Specified in UNI 4.0.

leaky bucket—A technique for managing traffic flow. Packets (or cells) enter the bucket and are stored. They are transmitted from the bucket through a "calibrated leak" that transmits with the agreed traffic parameters. As long as the bucket doesn't overflow, cells can arrive in whatever size bursts happen to come, but as soon as it's full, cells (or packets) are discarded.

LEC—LAN Emulation Client.

LECS—LAN Emulation Configuration Server.

LES—LAN Emulation Server.

link—A connection between two entities that wish to communicate.

LIS—Logical IP Subnet.

listen—To await communication on a given link or channel.

MAC—Medium Access Control. The way a shared-medium network arbitrates which host will be able to transmit. Ethernet's CSMA/CD is one example.

MAC address—The address used at the MAC layer; an Ethernet address is an example.

MARS—Multicast Address Resolution Server. RFC 2022's server for ATM multicast.

Mbone—Multicast Backbone. The collection of networks and mrouters that form the Internet's experimental multicast network.

MCR—Minimum Cell Rate.

MIB—Management Information Base. The hierarchy of data items defined for SNMP.

MMF—Multimode Fiber.

MPEG—Motion Picture Experts Group, also the standard for compressed digital video developed by them.

mrouter—A multicast router that implements multicast routing protocols, honors join and prune messages, and provides tunnels for nonmulticast capable network links.

MSL—Maximum Segment Lifetime.

MSS—Maximum Segment Size. The largest segment that can be transmitted for a given TCP connection.

MTA—Mail Transfer Agent. A program that transfers electronic mail between computers and saves it in user's mailboxes, often without human intervention. Distinct from a MUA (q.v.)

MUA—Mail User Agent. A program used by humans to read and send electronic mail. Distinct from an MTA (q.v.)

Multicast—The technique of sending one packet to multiple destinations.

Multicast Cluster—A group of computers implementing RFC 2022-style multicast over ATM.

Multicast Forward VCC—The unidirectional point-to-multipoint virtual connection over which a LANE BUS sends multicast packets to its clients.

multicast group—The set of computers participating in a given multicast session.

Multicast Send VCC—The unidirectional point-to-point virtual connection over which a LANE client sends multicast packets to the BUS.

nameserver—A host that implements the DNS (Domain Name Service) protocol to resolve domain names like "www.foo.com" into IP addresses (12.34.56.78).

NBMA—Nonbroadcast Multiple Access; a class of networks characterized by multiple access (many hosts can access the net simultaneously) and a lack of broadcast capability (i.e., it is not possible to send a packet that will be received by all hosts).

NDIS—Network Driver Interface Specification; an interface defined for IBM/PC network cards.

network—A group of computers connected together so as to transmit and receive information. Also, the technology used to perform the connecting.

NHRP—Next Hop Routing Protocol. The IETF scheme for providing shortcut routing across NBMA networks.

NHS—Next Hop Server. The server in a LIS that provides NHRP services.

node—A device functioning as part of a network. Distinct from a *link*, which connects nodes.

NTSC—National Television System Committee. The television standard used in the United States, Canada, and Japan. Does *not* stand for "Never Twice the Same Color."

Object Identifier—A hierarchical sequence of numbers used to identify managed objects for SNMP.

octet—Eight bits. A byte on all but the weirdest antique computers.

OID—An Object Identifier.

OSI—Open Systems Interconnect. The ISO attempt to design a suite of network protocols. Mostly dead in the face of the Internet's robust and explosive growth.

OUI—Organizationally Unique Identifier, a number assigned by ISO to identify protocol standardizing bodies.

packet—A chunk of data sent across a network as a single unit.

PAL—Phase Alternating Line, the European (except for France) Television standard.

PARC—Palo Alto Research Center, CA. One of Xerox' research labs.

PC—Personal Computer. In 1997, an IBM-compatible computer running Microsoft Windows. In historic usage, any computer dedicated to a single user. Xerox PARC's ALTO has a good claim to being the first.

PCR—Peak Cell Rate.

PDU—Protocol Data Unit. "Internationastandardscommitteespeak" for packet.

Peer—A peer of a given entity is another entity at the same level of operation. In ATM terms it's often "The box on the other end of this fiber here." Thus, the peer of an end station will be the switch it's connected to, and the peers of a switch will be the other switches and end stations it is connected to.

PID—Protocol Identifier. A number used to identify the protocol in MARS.

ping—Program that sends ICMP Echo-Request packets to a host and reports if Echo-Replies come back. Extremely useful for diagnosing network problems.

point-to-multipoint—A network connection from one computer to one or more other computers.

point-to-point—A network connection from one computer to exactly one other computer.

Poisson Distribution—A mathematical model of events used in (among others) network simulation.

Policing—The practice of enforcing Quality of Service limits.

POP—Post Office Protocol, a protocol used by MUAs and MTAs to talk to each other. Also Point of Presence, an installation by a public network in a locality to provide local access for customers.

ports—A connection on an ATM switch. Also, a number used in IP to indicate which of many programs on a computer should receive data in a given packet.

Prodigy—A large on-line network provider.

protocol stack—The software to implement a suite of network protocols; consisting of the hardware device drivers, the protocol modules, and the application programs. Called a stack because the pieces "stack" up, like the OSI layers.

PSH—The TCP "Push" flag; used to force immediate transmission of data; more or less obsolete.

QoS—Quality of Service. The collection of parameters (peak and average data rate, delay tolerance, jitter tolerance) that indicate what acceptable quality is for a given connection.

queue—A line of items waiting for service.

queuing theory—Mathematical theory dealing with queues.

RFC—Request for Comments; working documents of the IETF.

RM—Resource Management. A type of cell used in ATM-latter OAM.

ROM—Read-Only memory; computer memory that cannot be written to, only read from.

root node—In a hierarchical arrangement of nodes, the one at the base is called the "root" node, in analogy to a tree trunk springing from the ground and branching out repeatedly until the twigs terminate in leaves.

router—A specialized computer that processes packets and determines the best link to transmit them on so as to get them to their destination. Pronounced either "rowter" or "rooter." Holy wars have been fought over this. Personally, I tend to unconsciously switch depending on how the person I'm talking to does it.

route—A rule for a router to use to determine the best path for a given packet.

routing table—A table of routes stored in a router.

RPC—Remote Procedure Call.

RST—The TCP RESET flag. Sent to abort a TCP connection.

RSVP—Resource ReSerVation Protocol. The IETF scheme for guaranteed resource allocation in the Internet.

SAAL—Signaling AAL. The AAL used in UNI signaling.

SEAL—Simple and Efficient Adaptation Layer. What AAL5 was called before it was accepted as a standard.

SECAM—The French acronym for Sequential Color with Memory.

Segment—A portion of a TCP stream, usually sent as a single packet in the absence of fragmentation.

Sender-initiated join—A technique for managing multipoint virtual circuits wherein only the sender (i.e., initiator of the circuit) can add new receivers to the connection.

sequence numbers—TCP numbers the bytes in a transmission sequentially and labels each packet with the sequence number of the first byte of data. Used to ensure reliable transport of data.

server—A computer or program that provides a service; typically passively waits for connections from clients, accepts requests for service, and sends back replies.

session announcements—Messages announcing multicast "sessions" are sent periodically on a well-known multicast address; they contain the information needed for a party to "join" or participate in the session.

shaping—The practice of regulating data flow in accordance with certain parameters.

SMF—Single-Mode Fiber.

sliding window protocol—A protocol in which an adjustable range of data (the "window") is eligible for transmission at any given time. Flow control will adjust the size and position of the window in the data stream.

SMDS—Switched Multi-Megabit Data Service.

SMTP—Simple Mail Transfer Protocol.

SNAP—Subnetwork Access Point.

SNMP—Simple Network Management Protocol. The Internet protocol used for managing network devices.

SONET—Synchronous Optical Network. A data communications technology used by telephone companies and by ATM in the USA and Canada. Similar to SDH in the rest of the world.

SSCOP—Service Specific Connection Oriented Protocol. Defined in ITU Recommendation Q.2110, used for transport of UNI signaling messages.

switch—A device that forwards packets. Similar to a router but operates at a lower layer of the protocol stack.

SYN—The TCP Synchronize flag. Sent in the first packet of a connection to indicate that this *is* the first packet.

Taylor series—A way of representing mathematical functions by an infinite polynomial sum. Often easier to work with than the original function, despite the infinite sum business. If I had a dime for every time one of my physics profs said "...and we can neglect the higher order terms"....

TCP/IP—Transmission Control Protocol/Internet Protocol. The Internet protocol suite and the two most widely used of its protocols.

Telnet—An early (and still used) Internet protocol for providing command-line access to remote computers.

TLA—Three-Letter Acronym. There are far too many TLAs and FLAs. In fact, considering that there are only 17,576 possible TLAs, we may be facing a worldwide shortage.

TLV—Type-Length-Value, a flexible method of encoding data used in SNMP, ILMI and MARS (and more...).

Tragedy of the Commons—When people can graze their cattle on the common field for no cost, too many cattle will be placed there, and the field will become overgrazed and rendered useless to all.

UBR—Unspecified Bit Rate.

UDP—User Datagram Protocol.

UNI—User/Network Interface; the interface between a host or user computer and the ATM network.

UNI 3.1—A specification of the UNI promulgated by the ATM Forum and widely implemented in ATM LAN Equipment.

unicast—Traditional one-sender, one-receiver data transmission, a back-formation from broadcast.

URG—The TCP Urgent flag, indicating high priority data is present in the stream.

VBR—Variable Bit Rate.

VC—Virtual Circuit. A communication channel that may share a physical medium with other VCs and provides sequential delivery of ATM cells.

VCC—Virtual Channel Connection. A unidirectional sequence of Virtual Channel Links between endpoints.

VCI—Virtual Circuit Identifier. A number assigned to a VC to distinguish its cells from those of other circuits. Does not have end-to-end significance.

VCL—Virtual Channel Link. A connection between two pieces of ATM gear; a part of a VCC.

VP—A logical group of VCs that can be switched as a unit.

VPI—Virtual Path Indicator. A number assigned to a VP. Does not have end-to-end significance.

WAN—Wide Area Network. A network that spans a geographically "large" area.

WWW—World Wide Web. The group of servers using the Hypertext Transfer Protocol to implement a flexible easy-to-use information service on the Internet.

X—A Window System in wide use on Unix workstations.

XNS—Xerox Network Services. A suite of networking protocols, first used on the original Ethernet. Ancestor to IPX.

Bibliography

Armitage, G., *Support for Multicast Over UNI 3.0/3.1 Based ATM Networks*, RFC 2022, Nov. 1996.

Atkinson, R. *Default IP MTU for Use Over ATM AAL5*, RFC 1626, May 1994.

ATM Forum, 1994, *PNNI Draft Specification.* ATM Forum 94-0471R13.

ATM Forum, 1994a, *ATM Physical Medium Dependent Interface Specification for 155 Mb/s Over Twisted Pair Cable*, AF-PHY-0015.000.

ATM Forum, 1996, *Interim Local Management Interface (ILMI) Specification Version 4.0*, AF-ILMI-0065.000.

ATM Forum, 1997a, *LAN Emulation over ATM Version 2—LUNI Specification.* AF-LANE-0084.000, July 1997.

ATM Forum, 1997b, *Multi-Protocol Over ATM Version 1.0,* AF-MPOA-0087.000, July 1997.

Berc, Lance, "A BAGNet Reality Check," *Hot Interconnects*, Stanford, CA, 1995. Also at
    http://chocolate.research.digital.com/hoti95/talk.html

Borsook, P., "On location with the masters of the metaverse," *Wired* 3(10) 110-188.

Case, J. D., M. Fedor, M. L. Schoffstall, and C. Davin, *Simple Network Management Protocol (SNMP),* RFC 1157, 1990.

Casner, Stephen and Stephen Deering, "First IETF Internet Audiocast," *ACM SIGCOMM Comput. Commun. Rev.*, vol. 22, p. 3, July 1992.

Chu, Hsiao-keng Jerry, "Zero-Copy TCP in Solaris." *Proc. 1996 Winter Usenix Tech. Conf.*, San Diego.

Clark, D., S. Shenker, and L. Zhang. "Supporting real-time applications in an Integrated Services Packet Network: architecture and mechanism," *Proc. SIGCOMM '92*, Aug. 1992, pp. 14–26.

Cole, R, D. Shur, and C. Villamizar, *IP Over ATM: A Framework Document*, RFC 1932, 1996.

de Prycker, Martin, *Asynchronous Transfer Mode, Solution for Broadband IDSN*, Ellis Horwood, 1991.

Feller, W., *An Introduction to Probability Theory and its Applications, Vol. I*. Wiley, 1950.

Fowler, H. and W. Leland, "Local Area Network traffic characteristics, with Implications for broadband network congestion management," *IEEE J. Select. Areas Commun.*, vol. SAC-9, no. 7, pp. 1139–1149, Sept. 1991.

Green, P. E., *Fiber Optic Networks*, Prentice-Hall, Englewood Cliffs, NJ, 1993.

Guthrie, A., *Alice's Restaurant,* Warner Brothers Records, 1967.

Hammond, J. L, J. E. Brown, and S. S. Liu, "Development of a transmission error model and an error control model," Tech. Rep. RADC-TR-75-138, Rome Air Development Center, 1975.

Heinanen, Juha, *Multiprotocol Encapsulation Over ATM Adaptation Layer 5*, RFC 1483, July 1993.

Jacobson, Van, *Tutorial Notes from SIGCOMM '90*, Philadelphia, Sept. 1990.

Jacobsen, Van, "Congestion avoidance and control," *Proc. ACM SIGCOMM '88*, Stanford, CA, Aug. 1988, pp. 54–64.

Jacobson, Van, R. Braden, and D. Bormanm, *TCP Extensions for High Performance*, RFC 1323, May 1992.

Johnston, Bill and Berry Kercheval, "BAGNet: A high speed, metropolitan area, ATM network," *Hot Interconnects*, Stanford, CA, Sept. 1994.

Kaufman, Charlie, R. Perlman, and M. Speciner, *Network Security; PRIVATE Communication in a PUBLIC World*, Prentice-Hall, 1995.

Kay, J. and J. Pasquale, "The importance of non-data touching processing overheads in TCP/IP," *Proc. ACM Commun. Architectures and Protocols Conf. (SIGCOMM)*, San Francisco, CA, Sept. 1993, pp. 259–269.

Kent, C. A. and J. C. Mogul, "Fragmentation considered harmful," *Proc. ACM SIGCOMM '87*, Stowe, VT, Aug. 11–13, 1987, pp. 390–401.

Kumar, Vinay, *MBone: Interactive Multimedia On The Internet*, Macmillan, New York, Nov. 1995.

Laubach, Mark and Berry Kercheval, "Bay Area broadband testbeds and technology," *INET 94 Proc.*, Prague, Czech Republic, June 1994.

Laubach, Mark, *Classical IP Over ATM*, RFC 1577, 1994.

Lefelhocz, Christopher, Bryan Lyles, Scott Shenker, and Lixia Zhang, "Congestion control for best-effort service: why we need a new paradigm," *IEEE Network Mag.*, vol. 10, no. 1, Jan./Feb. 1996.

Leland, Will E., Murad S. Taqqu, Walter Willinger, Daniel V. Wilson, "On the self-similar nature of Ethernet traffic (extended version)," *IEEE/ACM Trans. Networking*, vol. 2, no. 1,pp. 1–15, Feb. 1994.

Lidl, Jurt, J. Osborne, and Joseph Malcolm, "Drinking from the firehose: Multicast USENET news," *USENIX Winter 1994 Tech. Conf. Proc.*, San Francisco, CA, Jan. 17–21, 1994.

Luciani, James V., Dave Katz, David Piscitello, and Bruce Cole, *NBMA Next Hop Resolution Protocol (NHRP)*, Internet draft (work in progress).

Lyles, J, Bryan and Christoph L. Schuba, "A reference model for firewall technology and its implications for connection signaling," *Proc. Open Signaling Workshop*, Columbia University, New York, NY, Oct. 1996.

Lyon, T., *Simple and Efficient Adaptation Layer (SEAL)*, ANSI T1S1.5/91-292, 1991.

Merkle, Ralph, "Secure communication over insecure channels," *Commun. ACM*, vol. 2, pp. 294–299, Apr. 1978.

Miller, S., C. Neuman, J. Schiller, and J. Salzer, *Kerberos Authentication and Authorization System*, Project Athena Tech. Plan, Section E.2.1, MIT Project Athena, Cambridge MA, 1987.

Mogul, J. C. and S. E. Deering, 1990. *Path MTU Discovery*, RFC 1191.

Mogul, J. C. 1993. "IP network performance," in *Internet System Handbook*, D. C. Lynch and M. T. Rose, Eds., Addison-Wesley, Reading, MA, pp. 575–675.

Moldeklev, Kjersti and Per Gunningberg, "Deadlock situations in TCP over ATM," *4th Int. IFIP Workshop on Protocols for High Speed Networks*, Vancouver, Canada, Aug. 10–12, 1994.

Partridge, C., *Gigabit Networking*, Addison-Wesley, Reading, MA, 1994.

Paxson, Vern and Sally Floyd, "Wide-area traffic: the failure of Poisson modeling," Lawrence Berkeley Lab. Tech. Rep. LBL-35238, Aug. 1994. A shorter version of this paper appeared in Proc. *SIGCOMM '94*.

Perez, M., F. Liaw, D. Grossman, A. Mankin, E. Hoffman, and A. Malis, *ATM Signaling Support for IP over ATM*, RFC 1755, Feb. 1995.

Perlman, R., *Interconnections: Bridges and Routers*, Addison-Wesley, Reading, MA, 1992.

Postel, J., *Internet Protocol*, RFC 791, Sept. 1, 1981.

Plummer, D. C., *Ethernet Address Resolution Protocol: Or Converting Network Protocol Addresses to 48-bit Ethernet Address for Transmission on Ethernet Hardware*, RFC 826, 1982.

Quarterman. J. S., "User growth of the Internet and of the Matrix," *Matrix News*, vol. 6, no. 5, May 1996.

Ramsøy, Tor Jakob, "The governing structure of the Internet," Master's thesis, Massachusetts Institute of Technology, Cambridge, MA.

Rose, Marshall, *The Simple Book,* 2nd ed., Prentice-Hall, Upper Saddle River, NJ, 1996.

Savetz, K., N. Randall, and Y. Lepage, *MBone: Multicasting Tomorrow's Internet*. IDG Books, Worldwide, Foster City, CA, 1996.

Scheifler, Robert, *X Window System*, Digital Press, Newton, MA, 1992.

Schuba, Christoph, J., Bryan Lyles, and Eugene H. Spafford, "A reference model for firewall technology," *SPARTAN Symp.*, Univ. of Kansas, Lawrence, Mar. 1997.

Schuba, Christoph, Berry Kercheval, and Eugene H. Spafford, "Prototyping experiences with IP over ATM," *J. of Sys. Software*, to appear, 1998.

Stevens, W. R., *TCP/IP Illustrated*, Addison-Wesley, Reading, MA, 1994.

Thadani, Moti, N. Thadani, and Yousef A. Khalidi, *An Efficient Zero-Copy I/O Framework for UNIX. Sun Microsys. Lab. Tech. Rep.* TR-95-39, May 1995.

Waitzman, D. *Standard for the Transmission of IP Datagrams on Avian Carriers*, RFC 1149, Apr. 1, 1990.

Yang, Cui-Qing and Alapti V. S. Reddy, "A taxonomy of congestion control algorithms in packet switching networks," *IEEE Network Mag.*, vol. 9, no. 5, July/Aug. 1995.

Index